Praise for
The CBT Toolbox for Young Adults

"Once again, Dr. Phifer takes us from *why* and gives us the *how*. *The CBT Toolbox for Young Adults* provides a ready and valuable resource for the early career to advanced practitioner."

—**Eric Rossen, PhD, NCSP,** psychologist and author of *Supporting and Educating Traumatized Students: A Guide for School-Based Professionals, 2nd Edition*

"*The CBT Toolbox for Young Adults* is a must-have! The skill-building activities provide clinicians with tools to capitalize on clients' strengths. Dr. Weed Phifer's latest toolbox will not disappoint."

—**Jessica Dirsmith, DEd, NCSP,** clinical assistant professor, licensed psychologist, and co-author of *Assessment and Identification of Students with Emotional Disturbance and Behavioral Needs*

"*The CBT Toolbox for Young Adults* is essential for everyone coaching young adults towards their next steps in life. The activities are thoughtfully designed and scaffolded to promote consistent skill growth and foster independence. This affirming lens ensures that activities can be tailored to the unique profile of each individual. I am excited to incorporate these essential tools in the future."

—**Laura K. Sibbald, MA, CCC-SLP, ASDCS, CYMHS,** associate director of Disability Resources and Neurodiversity Initiatives at Chestnut Hill College, and co-author of *Trauma-Informed Social-Emotional Toolbox for Children & Adolescents* and *Parenting Toolbox*

"*The CBT Toolbox for Young Adults* provides functional activities to help prepare youth for adulthood. It includes easy-to-use tools for both clients and clinicians!"

—**Bethany Demers, MA, CAS,** mental wellness specialist

"As a parent of two teenagers, I find this workbook incredibly helpful in teaching our kids healthy habits to manage the excitement and stress that comes with independence."

—**Erika Dronen,** parent

The
CBT
Toolbox
for Young Adults

170 Tools for Coping with Stress,
Building Healthy Habits &
Navigating Adulthood

LISA WEED PHIFER, DEd, NCSP

The CBT Toolbox for Young Adults
Copyright © 2022 by Lisa Weed Phifer

Published by:
PESI Publishing, Inc.
3839 White Ave.
Eau Claire, WI 54703

Cover: Amy Rubenzer
Editing: Jenessa Jackson, PhD
Layout: Baker & Taylor and Amy Rubenzer

ISBN: 9781683734710 (print)
ISBN: 9781683734727 (ePUB)
ISBN: 9781683734734 (ePDF)

PESI Publishing
pesipublishing.com

Table of Contents

Chapter 2
Anxiety

Chapter 3
Depression

Chapter 4
Traumatic Stress

Chapter 5
Attention-Deficit/ Hyperactivity Disorder

Chapter 6
Autism Spectrum Disorder

Chapter 7
Anger and Related Behavior Disorders

Introduction

Many adolescents long for the days of freedom and independence typically associated with the transition to adulthood. But what does it truly mean to be an adult? Being an adult is much more than just an age; it comes with responsibilities, excitement, and challenges. As young adults strive to create their own identity, they must learn to express their thoughts in meaningful ways, form relationships, adjust to changing situations, and persevere during challenging times. When this transition is coupled with mental health issues, it's important for individuals to have strategies they can use to empower themselves and regain control. *The CBT Toolbox for Young Adults* is designed to support the needs of this critical age group by providing a compilation of these very strategies. Using a cognitive behavioral therapy approach, this toolbox is composed of solution-focused therapeutic ideas to enhance the coping abilities of young adults as they tackle life's major hurdles.

In this toolbox, young adults will find over 170 engaging activities to develop self-awareness, harness their unique strengths, and learn healthy ways to adapt to their changing worlds. These activities will help young readers better understand stress, recognize triggers, and apply coping tools to support general wellness. Additionally, this toolbox provides numerous opportunities to identify and reframe faulty thinking patterns that can negatively cloud their view of themselves and the world. Finally, important life skills are woven throughout each section that support individuals in developing effective work habits, balancing personal and professional obligations, and forming healthy relationships.

These activities focus on creating healthy physical, mental, and social habits that enhance independence as readers learn to:

- Understand the relationship between their thoughts, feelings, and behaviors

- Foster a positive attitude and mindset

- Develop problem-solving strategies to adjust to and manage life's challenges

- Build self-advocacy skills

- Strengthen their relationship skills

Who Is This Book For?

Calling all coaches! This toolbox is designed for clinicians who are working with young adults to guide them in developing and strengthening social-emotional and life skills that are critical for success in adulthood. Although this book is clinically focused, it can also be used by parents or other coaches who are supporting young adults in their transition to adulthood. Activities can be tailored to each client's needs to assist them in developing new routines that promote financial and personal independence and real-life problem solving.

This book also includes self-coaching tools that young adults can complete independently or as carryover activities between sessions.

What Is in This Book

The book is divided into seven areas—Adulting, Anxiety, Depression, Traumatic Stress, Attention-Deficit/ Hyperactivity Disorder, Autism Spectrum Disorder, and Anger and Related Behavior Disorders—with a variety of activities in each area to support psychoeducation, healthy thinking patterns, resiliency building, relationship coaching, and mindfulness. Many of these activities cover the following themes:

- **Critical life skill** activities help clients learn routines for independence, balance personal and professional obligations, and prioritize needs.

- **Symptom recognition** activities help clients learn how their strengths and challenges impact them at work, at home, and in relationships.

- **Cognitive reframing** activities teach clients how to identify and reframe maladaptive thoughts in a way that supports healthy thoughts, feelings, and behaviors.

- **Relationship coaching** activities teach clients the social skills necessary to build and maintain healthy relationships, such as boundary setting, perspective taking, and building trust.

- **Resiliency building** activities provide coping and self-advocacy strategies to strengthen clients' ability to self-regulate and problem solve.

- **Mindful learning** activities help clients tune in to the mind-body connection, practice self-care, and establish and maintain healthy habits.

How to Use This Book

Although this book is not a treatment manual, it contains activities that therapists can easily integrate into their clinical practice when working with young adults. Many activities also contain carryover ideas that clients can practice in real-life situations outside of the therapy office, such as home, school, work, or other social settings. Therapists should feel free to use the activities that best fit each client's goals and that align with the scope of their professional practice. The following activities are included throughout this book:

 In-session exercises are designed for the therapist to use with the client in session. These activities may introduce new skills and are intended to engage the client and allow them to practice the targeted skill.

 Client activities encourage clients to apply the skills they have learned and to practice problem-solving techniques on their own, either inside or outside the session, to enhance carryover and build self-efficacy.

 Homework assignments support clients in generalizing the skills they have learned in session to the real world. For example, clients might be asked to track their mood or coping habits, create schedules, or try new routines.

Throughout this book, clients will be asked to explore and implement a variety of coping tools to address everyday issues and problem solve during times of major stress. Coping tools are a wide range of strategies that help calm the body and mind so individuals can manage their feelings and actions in helpful ways. These tools strengthen self-awareness, build resiliency during challenging times, and reduce stress by helping clients focus on what is within their control.

It is important to continuously adjust coping tools to match the individual's comfort level, the intensity of the situation, and other situational factors (whether the client is at work versus home, whether they have access to supports, and so on). There are many coping ideas to try, so here is a list to consider throughout this book.

Coping Skills To...			
Calm the Body and Mind	**Engage the Body and Mind**	**Connect with Others**	**Create a Positive Mindset**
• Adjust lighting to create a calming effect • Listen to calming music or sounds • Visualize success when faced with an upcoming challenge • Visualize a favorite memory or calming place • Count forward to or backward from 100 • Do a guided breathing activity • Find a relaxing, quiet space to decompress • Use aromatherapy • Create to-do lists to reduce worry	• Cook or bake • Play an instrument • Do some knitting or crocheting • Write a song, poem, or story • Journal about your experiences • Create your own stress ball or fidget spinner • Try out an adult coloring book • Get your body moving by going for a brisk walk or jog	• Reach out a loved one • Share your feelings with others • Ask for help or advice from a trusted person • Call a friend or family member after a hard day • Create healthy boundaries with others to reduce stress • Use humor to ease tense situations	• Reflect on your personal values to help guide you in a situation • Reframe negative or unhelpful thoughts • Set positive intentions • Recognize your personal strengths during times of doubt or challenge • Think about positive events in the future • Intentionally focus on the present rather than past actions • Focus on what you can control in a situation (your thoughts, feelings, actions, and words)

Interject creativity when possible, allowing clients to journal, draw, and reflect upon the skills they have learned and the progress they have made. Consider pairing the tools found in this book with hands-on experiences, and practice modeling the skills through video or role-plays to further strengthen the carryover of skills. And always remember to acknowledge your efforts. This is hard yet rewarding work as you help youth navigate this big life transition. Let's get coaching!

Adulting

Welcome, young adults and clinicians! Independence is right around the corner, but there is much work to do. This chapter helps clients embrace their upcoming transition to adulthood as they establish their values and ideals of being self-sufficient and set goals for success. Initial activities provide creative ideas for in-session work that clinicians can use to structure sessions and build rapport with clients. Given that each person brings their own experiences and strengths to the table, the activities in this chapter will help clinicians and clients focus on existing skill sets and work together to navigate upcoming changes and challenges.

As you read through this chapter, you'll find activities that help define clients' views, values, and goals for the future. Practical activities are also included that highlight the skills needed for clients to live on their own, gain financial independence, and develop healthy habits. The chapter concludes with goal-setting strategies to help clients set and reach personal goals throughout this journey. Clinicians should periodically review goals and achievements and adapt tools as necessary to meet clients' needs.

Client Session Agenda

Use this agenda during your session to help you take notes as necessary and to track your growth.

Date of session: _____

I. Check-In
- How are you feeling today?

Upset	Worried	Okay	Happy	Great	Other

II. Last Time
- Review of last session and homework
- Anything notable since last session? _____

III. Today's Objectives
- _____
- _____
- _____

IV. Next Time
- Review homework

V. End of Session Check-In
- Summary of today's work
- Thank you for your efforts!
- How do you feel at the end of the session?

Upset	Worried	Okay	Happy	Great	Other

Clinician Session Agenda

Use this agenda to help structure your sessions, take relevant notes, and collect information to support your client's progress.

Client name: _____

Date of session: _____

I. Check-In
- How does the client feel today?

    Upset   Worried   Okay   Happy   Great   Other: _____

II. Last Time
- Review of last session and homework
- Anything notable since last session? _____

III. Today's Objectives
- _____
- _____
- _____
- Notes: _____

IV. Next Time
- Review homework
- Other important notes: _____

V. End of Session Check-In
- Summarize the session
- Check in with the client about how they feel at the end of the session

    Upset   Worried   Okay   Happy   Great   Other: _____

What's in Your Coping Toolbox?

Coping tools are strategies that help you keep focused, stay in control, and manage uncomfortable feelings like stress, worry, or anger. Successful coping strategies help you release energy so you can handle a situation to the best of your abilities.

What helps you keep your cool in tough situations, like when your boss tells you disappointing news or when a friend breaks your trust? Use this worksheet to list the coping tools you have found to be helpful in these types of situations. List as many or as few tools as you find helpful. You can also continue to record additional skills as you learn them. Try writing in different colors as you add more skills, or make notes about situations in which the tools work best.

Calming Tools	Creative Tools	Physically Active Tools	Positive Mindset Tools	Other Helpful Tools
Examples: *deep breathing, visualization, meditation*	Examples: *painting, journaling, singing*	Examples: *running, biking, moving*	Examples: *starting a positive intention, practicing gratitude, focusing on strengths*	

How's It Going? Coping Check-In

In-Session Exercise

Use this worksheet to check in with how you are feeling and to record any notable changes or events since the last session. Then list any coping skills you are currently using and indicate whether they are helping you stay in control. Finally, identify potential coping skills that might be helpful in dealing with upcoming stressors.

1. Coping Check-In

1	2	3	4	5
No stress	Little stress	Manageable stress	Stressed	Very stressed

2. Current Coping Tools

What tools have you been using? Are they helping?

Current Coping Tools	Helpful?		
	Yes	Maybe	No

3. Upcoming Events

Are there any upcoming events that may be stressful? If so, what other coping tools can you add to your list?

Upcoming Events	Coping Tools

Personal Case Management

This is a quick reference tool that will help you organize your medical history and provider contact information. As you begin transitioning into adulthood, you become responsible for organizing all this personal information that once was taken care of by your caregivers. By completing this case management tool, you can have a quick reference sheet if you need to communicate with medical or clinical professionals on your own or in an emergency.

Medical and Clinical Information

Diagnoses: _____

Symptoms: _____

Known allergies: _____

Medications and schedule: _____

Provider*	Contact Number/Email	Treatment Schedule

*Physician, psychiatrist, psychologist, social worker, counselor, case manager, etc.

Other Important Contacts

Trusted adult, friend, or support person in case I need help:

    Name: _____

    Contact information: _____

What to do in case of an emergency:

    Name of local crisis unit or community resource: _____

    Contact information: _____

The Real Me Résumé

Express your true self by providing your unique information.

Preferred name/nickname: _____

Three words that best describe me: _____

A topic I know a lot about: _____

Something I'd like to learn more about: _____

My favorite way to relax on the weekend: _____

My activity of choice during my free time: _____

My go-to person when I'm upset: _____

My go-to person when I'm excited: _____

My ideal environment to learn: _____

My ideal job: _____

Something that I tried but did not do well at: _____

Something that I tried and did well at: _____

My favorite outfit to wear to school or work: _____

My favorite meal to make at home: _____

My favorite meal to order out: _____

A place that I would like to visit: _____

A moment that I am proud of: _____

Something that I would like to happen in the future: _____

My favorite quality about myself: _____

Something that really irritates me: _____

Something that really excites me: _____

When I think about the future, I feel: _____

Would You Rather?

To help you and your clinician get to know each other better, take turns asking each other some of the following "would you rather" questions. You can use the questions provided or come up with your own. You can also use these questions outside of session to lighten the mood and create a more comfortable environment when meeting new people.

Questions:

Would you rather create a podcast or a blog?

Would you rather stay up late or wake up early?

Would you rather read a book or read from an electronic device?

Would you rather complete a group project or an individual project?

Would you rather speak in front of others or share your thoughts on social media?

Would you rather draw pictures or take pictures?

Would you rather create music or listen to music?

Would you rather write down your grocery list or remember it in your head?

Would you rather eat dessert for breakfast or breakfast for dinner?

Would you rather text a friend or call a friend?

Would you rather play chess or soccer?

Would you rather arrive five minutes early or be right on time?

Would you rather know what comes next or be surprised?

Would you rather cry at a sad movie or cry at a funny joke?

Would you rather play a game or watch someone play a game?

Would you rather eat only vegetables or only meat?

Would you rather have summer all the time or winter all the time?

Would you rather share your feelings with others or keep them to yourself?

Would you rather learn from a mistake or avoid taking risks?

Five-Star Review

We each possess strengths when it comes to our ability to meet a deadline, to be dependable, to be trustworthy, or to be helpful. Knowing that our strengths shine in different settings, what about you deserves a five-star review? Put yourself in the shoes of your friends, family members, and mentors, and decide what they each would say about you that warrants five stars.

I give [*insert your name*] _____ a ★ ★ ★ ★ ★ review because

_____

_____

—Friend

I give [*insert your name*] _____ a ★ ★ ★ ★ ★ review because

_____

_____

—Family member

I give [*insert your name*] _____ a ★ ★ ★ ★ ★ review because

_____

_____

—Past teacher, coach, or supervisor

Quick Start

Complete this quick introductory activity to help you share a little bit more about yourself. Select a few or try them all.

I would describe myself as...

1. _____

2. _____

3. _____

I would not describe myself as...

1. _____

2. _____

3. _____

I can't imagine life without...

1. _____

2. _____

3. _____

If I could give three gifts to others, they would be...

1. _____

2. _____

3. _____

If I were stranded on an island, I would bring...

1. _____

2. _____

3. _____

What's App?

Phones and other devices have many creative apps that entertain us, keep us connected with friends and family, and help us stay organized. What apps do you like the most or check most frequently? In this activity, create your own app, icon included, that best describes your talents. For example, you might choose to develop a calendar app because you like to stay organized, a music app because you enjoy how music creates different moods, or an exercise app because you love being active.

App name: _____

What is it used for? _____

_____

_____

In what ways is this app helpful? _____

_____

_____

Write a review of your app: _____

_____

_____

Draw your app's icon here:

In-Session
Exercise

New Transitions Checklist

What does it take to be a successful adult? There are many skills to consider and opportunities to strive for when working toward the independence that comes with adulthood. This checklist includes an overview of skills relevant to adult living (though it is by no means exhaustive). Review this list with your clinician to guide your questioning of strengths and needs. Using the statements provided (and adding your own as you see fit), take note of what you already can do (+) and what you might need to work toward (o). This information can be helpful in planning for targeted skills and setting goals to support independence.

+	o	Self-Advocacy Skills
		I know my strengths.
		I know my challenges, weaknesses, or disabilities.
		I know how to communicate my needs to others.
		I can identify my values, morals, and limits.
		I know how to ask for help.
		Other:

+	o	Daily Living Skills
		I know how to safely live on my own or with others.
		I can purchase and safely prepare food.
		I know how to find a place to live.
		I know how to clean and organize my space.
		I can identify, budget, and pay for rent, utilities, and other necessary expenses.
		I know how to create a schedule for work, leisure, and other responsibilities.
		I make daily personal hygiene (e.g., brushing hair, brushing teeth, showering) a priority.
		I can select appropriate attire for work and casual settings.
		I know how to do laundry.
		Other:

+	o	Personal Health and Safety Skills
		I know and can manage my health needs.
		I know the names of my doctors and other providers.
		I know my health history and have access to my records.
		I know how to schedule and plan for appointments.
		I know basic first aid.
		I know what do to in case of an emergency, like call 911 or seek medical attention.
		Other:

+	o	Social and Leisure Skills
		I can find and engage in leisure activities and hobbies.
		I know how to make and maintain friendships.
		I can stay true to myself and make friends.
		I know how to apologize when I have made a mistake.
		I respect others' views and opinions.
		Other:

+	o	Self -Management Skills
		I can identify my feelings.
		I can manage my feelings.
		I know my triggers and how to manage or avoid them.
		I have coping strategies to stay in control.
		I practice healthy self-care activities to maintain balance.
		Other:

+	o	Transportation Skills
		I know how to access different modes of transportation.
		I know how to locate bus or subway schedules and routes.
		I know how to schedule transportation if accessing a transportation program.
		I can use my own transportation.
		I plan on obtaining or currently have a driver's license. If not, I have a plan to meet the requirements for a state ID card.
		I can budget for insurance, parking, and maintenance of my vehicle.
		I have a backup plan for transportation (e.g., rideshare program, support person).
		Other:

+	o	Postsecondary Training Skills
		I know the training required to reach my career aspirations.
		I know how to find a training or postsecondary school-based program.
		I know how to apply to selected programs.
		I know how to budget for my education (e.g., applying for scholarships or loans, maintaining sufficient savings or income).
		I know how to create a schedule to balance school and other responsibilities or activities (e.g., work, leisure).
		I know whom or how to ask for help if I have questions about my program.
		Other:

+	o	Employment Skills
		I know the skills I need to get a job.
		I know that I may need to work to gain experience to obtain my career goals.
		I know what is required of me at work.
		I can manage my needs at work (e.g., communicate with others, accept feedback, cope with stress).
		I know whom or how to ask for clarification or assistance while at my job.
		Other:

Defining Adult

Becoming an adult can be puzzling sometimes. The transition to adulthood brings about new freedoms and responsibilities as you begin navigating the world independently. Fill in the puzzle pieces with your thoughts of what it means to become an adult.

New Freedoms

New Responsibilities

Most Excited For

Most Concerned About

Past and Present

Transitioning into adulthood is a big deal. There are so many changes, new responsibilities, and exciting things to look forward to. Each of our stories is different, filled with accomplishments, setbacks, and challenges. Take a few minutes to reflect on your journey up to this point, and then envision where you would like to go. Where will the future take you? What goals would you like to accomplish? Use the timelines here to highlight any significant events that happened in the past, as well as those that you'd like to see happen in the future.

Reflect on the Past

- What are your proudest accomplishments (big or small)?

_____

_____

- Who are the people who supported you (e.g., family, friends, teachers, coaches)?

_____

_____

- What personal habits or skills helped you to be successful?

_____

_____

Envision Where You Want to Go

- Career aspirations: _____

_____

- Personal dreams: _____

_____

- What skills will you need? _____

_____

- Whom do you want around you? _____

_____

Core Values

We all have core character values that are important to us. They drive our actions, thoughts, and feelings as we try to present the best version of ourselves at home, school, and work. Values also differ from person to person. For example, one person may value being dependable, always showing up on time, and being there to support others. Another person may value being confident, facing challenges head-on, and trying new things. It's our unique combination of values that shapes our view of ourselves, others, and the world. Use this activity to highlight your own core values. Some values to consider include loyalty, integrity, honesty, or faith. Then think of ways that you can express these values at school, at work, with family, or with friends.

Display your values on the banner here:

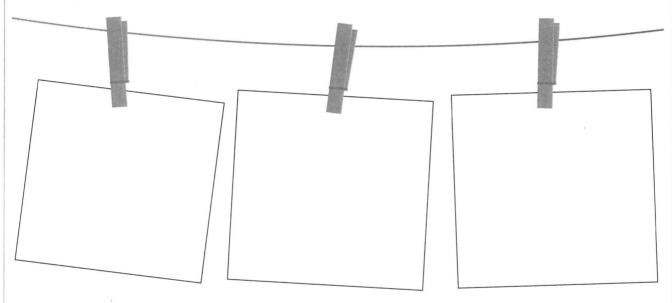

How can you show your core values through your actions with others in different settings? Think about what might be the same across settings and what might need to change to meet the needs of a different group of people (e.g., friends vs. coworkers).

I can show my values with my family members by: _____

_____

I can show my values with my colleagues at school or work by: _____

_____

I can show my values with my friends by: _____

_____

Examining *Why*

As you move through your journey toward developing a stronger mindset, set an intention that will keep you on your path. Define the motivation (or *why*) for this journey. *Why* are you setting goals? *Why* are you building skills? *Why* are you making your physical and mental health a priority? In the first box, describe why you are motivated to grow and learn more.

Once you have described your *why*, choose a word that reminds you of this intention. For example, perhaps you choose a word like *strong, change, grace, grow, welcome, embrace, support, develop, improve,* or *progress*. This word might even come from your *why* statement. Write this word in the second box, and design it as your personal logo. Display this word on your mirror at home, on your phone wallpaper, or on your laptop—any place highly visible to remind you of your *why*.

Describe your *why*:

Design your *why*:

Examples:

Strong   Grace

Message in a Bottle

Imagine you could write a letter to your future self, put it a bottle, and cast it to sea. Fast forward 10 years later: You're walking along the same beach and notice your bottle wash ashore. What does this message say? What advice did you give yourself? What dreams did you hope to have accomplished? Who did you hope would be around you? How do you view the world and others around you?

Adulting Bingo

Adulting means to behave in an adult manner. This fun bingo game will help you learn how to adult in a fun and lighthearted way. Cover each space as you complete the task or challenge. Good luck!

A	D	U	L	T
Showed gratitude to someone around you	Busy day tomorrow—chose to stay in rather than go out with friends	Exercised for 30 minutes a day, three times a week	Helped tackle chores, like doing laundry, making meals, and cleaning	Asked for help when you needed it
Skipped the coffee shop and made coffee at home instead	Used a planner or calendar to keep track of your to-dos	Prioritized work over fun (e.g., finished your to-do list before hanging out with friends)	Made it to school or work on time all week	Created a weekly budget
Engaged in reading, journaling, or another mindful activity for at least 30 minutes	Prepped for the next day before going to bed (e.g., packed your lunch, organized your bag)	**Free space**	Made a healthy meal	Finished a school or work project on time
Made a grocery list and stuck to it	Called a family member or friend to say hello	Helped a friend or family member	Created a weekly goal	Accomplished a weekly goal
Cleaned up your area at home and work at the end of the day	Set up autopay for a bill	Drank at least six glasses of water a day	Took a break from social media for the day	Went for a walk to clear your mind

Must-Dos

Each of us has tasks that we need to accomplish daily or weekly. These tasks include those related to work, school, health, hygiene, self-care, socializing, and leisure. Learning to prioritize these tasks is an important life skill for independence, as you must learn to balance those more urgent and important tasks (known as "must-dos") with other activities that bring you joy (known as "like-to-dos"). What are your daily and weekly must-dos and like-to-dos? Create a list that will help you build a routine.

Daily Must-Dos

_____

_____

_____

_____

_____

_____

Daily Like-to-Dos

_____

_____

_____

_____

_____

_____

Weekly Must-Dos

_____

_____

_____

_____

_____

_____

Weekly Like-to-Dos

_____

_____

_____

_____

_____

_____

Setting Limits

Setting healthy boundaries is a necessary coping strategy in adulthood. Balancing personal, social, education, and work commitments can be very stressful when you have tasks to get done and fun things you want to do. For this activity, think about how your schedule differs on work or school days compared to your days off. Then create tentative times when you can engage in the following activities and set limits for others. This will help you plan and balance your daily schedule.

Activity	Work/School Day	Day Off
Daily tasks (e.g., cleaning, laundry, errands)		
Relaxation and rest		
Social time		
Self-care and exercise		
Mealtime		
Responding to messages (e.g., emails, calls)		
Social media		
Other:		
Other:		
Other:		

Daily Schedule

Consistency and structure are important as you gain more independence. Use this template to create a daily schedule that will help you establish healthy habits and balance work and life demands. You can complete a different schedule for your work or school days versus your days off. As you complete your schedule, think about getting enough sleep, exercising, eating nourishing meals, completing work tasks, making time for hobbies and relaxation, and spending time with friends and family.

Time	Work/School Day	Day Off
12 a.m.–6 a.m.		
6 a.m.		
7 a.m.		
8 a.m.		
9 a.m.		
10 a.m.		
11 a.m.		
12 p.m.		
1 p.m.		
2 p.m.		
3 p.m.		
4 p.m.		
5 p.m.		
6 p.m.		
7 p.m.		
8 p.m.		
9 p.m.		
10 p.m.		
11 p.m.		

Weekday Wellness

Plan the week ahead the right way by prioritizing time each day to support your best self. In the following table, you'll find that each day has a wellness challenge. Read each description, and then create your own Weekday Wellness Plan.

	Weekday Wellness Plan
Self-Reflection Sunday	Set your intentions for the week. What do you want to accomplish?
Mindful Monday	Make time to practice meditation, mindful breathing, or another activity that helps you connect with the present.
Trust Yourself Tuesday	Trust in the process. Write down a positive affirmation and post it somewhere you will see it. You've got this!
Workout Wednesday	Time to stretch your legs and get your heart pumping! Pick an activity, like going on a walk with friends, taking a strength class, or practicing yoga. Just make time to move.
Thoughtful Thursday	Practice gratitude for others by saying "thank you," calling a family member, or doing an act of kindness for someone else.
Freestyle Friday	Express your true self by connecting with your creative side. Cook a new recipe, bake a cake, paint, write a poem, or do another creative activity you enjoy.
Super Saturday	Wow, what a week! Make time for something you enjoy today, whether it's hanging out with friends, indulging in a delicious dessert, or reading a great book.

What's Your Weekday Wellness Plan?

Sunday: _____

Monday: _____

Tuesday: _____

Wednesday: _____

Thursday: _____

Friday: _____

Saturday: _____

Menu Planner Part 1

Planning your meals ahead of time is a simple routine that can help reduce weekday stress. It can guide your grocery shopping and help you map out easy meals for busier days. Menu planning can also help you stay on budget, especially on those nights when you're tempted to order takeout because you don't know what to make! Use this template to plan your meals for the upcoming week and then create your grocery list.

Day	Meals	Ingredients Needed
Sunday		
Monday		
Tuesday		
Wednesday		
Thursday		
Friday		
Saturday		

Menu Planning Part 2: Balanced List

Having a balanced diet can improve your energy level, mood, and overall health. After creating your menu for the week using the previous Meal Planner activity, use this worksheet to organize your grocery list into categories. Writing out your grocery list this way will help you plan a healthy, balanced diet, and it will save you time in the grocery store.

Vegetables	Fruits

Protein	Grains

Dairy	Snacks

Beverages	Other Items

What You Want vs. What You Need

Spending your hard-earned money on trendy sneakers or the newest technology can make you feel good in the moment, but when the funds are gone, so is the fun. Budgeting your money wisely can help you feel less stressed, reinforce positive spending habits, and help you eventually get those desired new shoes! The first step in creating a budget is to define your basic budget needs, as well as the "wants" that are important to you. You may be able to keep some wants in your regular budget, while others might require a little saving (e.g., if you want to go on vacation or buy a new television).

First, let's practice. In the example below, mark each item as a need or a want.

Need	Want	
◯	◯	Groceries
◯	◯	Housing (e.g., rent, dorm fees)
◯	◯	Gym membership
◯	◯	Utilities (e.g., gas, electric, internet)
◯	◯	Morning coffee run
◯	◯	Transportation (e.g., car, bus, train)
◯	◯	New clothes
◯	◯	Monthly subscriptions (e.g., music, TV)

Now make your own list. What are your specific needs, and what are some items you would like to have?

My Needs	My Wants

Weekly Spending

"Where did my paycheck go?" Good question—bills add up fast! Tracking your spending habits is a great way to see how and where you spend money. Over the next week, look at your daily spending and write down the expenses that occur. Take notice of everything, even the few dollars you spend on a cup of coffee or a space in the parking garage. Whatever it is, write it down.

Day	Amount	Expense (Item/Service)

Now review your weekly spending. Are there any habits you can change to save money?

_____

_____

_____

_____

Saving and Spending: Monthly Budget Tool

You worked hard for your paycheck! Use this budget tool to map out your current budget, taking into consideration the money you are making, your monthly costs, and your bottom line. Stretch your hard-earned dollars to reach your budget goals.

1. Determine your budget goals.

What would you like to save money for (e.g., a car, a house, your education, a vacation)?	
How much money do you need to save in order to make this happen?	

2. Calculate income and expenses.

A. Determine your monthly income.

Income Source(s)	$
Monthly take-home pay	
Additional income sources	
Total income	

B. Calculate your monthly expenses.

Monthly Expenses	$
Housing (e.g., rent, dorm fees)	
Utilities (e.g., water, electricity, internet, phone)	
Food	
Household supplies (e.g., cleaning products)	
Personal care (e.g., hygiene products, haircuts, clothing)	
Transportation (e.g., car maintenance, insurance, shared ride)	
Medical expenses	
Debts (e.g., car payment, loans, credit cards)	
Education (e.g., tuition, textbooks, supplies)	
Subscriptions (e.g., gym membership, video streaming)	
Other spending	
Total spending	

3. Subtract your monthly expenses from your monthly income.

Monthly income (total from 2A):	$_____
Monthly expenses (total from 2B):	−$_____
Bottom dollar—money saved toward your budget goals:	$_____

Is this enough to accomplish your goals? If not, what habits can you change so you can save for your goals (e.g., limiting coffee shop runs, dining in, reducing subscriptions to music or streaming services)?

_____

_____

_____

_____

Healthy Budget Tips

- Pay your bills on time! Use autopay when possible for your bills.

- Adjust your budget when finances change, like when you have a salary increase or a new expense.

- Set aside a day each week to quickly review your credit card or bank statements. This is an easy to way to monitor your spending and catch any errors.

Housing Plans

Moving into your own place is a huge step in independence. As you navigate what housing you would like and what you can afford, take some time to plan out the factors that are necessary to guide your search, such as location, size, safety, and roommates. Start by acknowledging the three factors that are most important to you, and then consider other factors associated with finding a place to live that meets your needs and budget.

Three factors that are most important to me when it comes to housing:

1. _____

2. _____

3. _____

Factors to Consider

What Can I Afford?
Rent, utilities, parking, fees, insurance, etc.

Location Needs
Proximity to work, transportation, friends, etc.

How Soon?

Size

Safety

Roommates?

Roommate Classifieds

Having a roommate can make living on your own more affordable and fun. However, selecting the right roommate is key. You must be able to live with this person, respect each other, and work together to prevent or resolve any problems. Before you begin your search, it's important to think about what type of roommate you would like. While you may not be able to fulfill every wish, it is important to set boundaries when it comes what you are willing to work with. Here are some questions to consider when looking for a roommate.

Know what you are looking for. What are a few traits you would like in a roommate?

_____

_____

_____

_____

What are things you might consider (e.g., pets, different schedules, guests visiting)?

_____

_____

_____

_____

What are your non-negotiables (e.g., habits like smoking, inconsistent jobs, opposite schedules)?

_____

_____

_____

_____

What is your experience with sharing a living space?

_____

_____

_____

_____

Roommate Interview

Here are some questions to ask your prospective roommate. Select questions that are important to you and add your own.

- What are you looking for in a roommate?

- Have you had roommates in the past?

- Are you employed?

- Do you pay your bills on time?

- What is your typical schedule when it comes to work, sleep, and so on?

- How often do you expect to have visitors?

- What your feelings about overnight visitors?

- How often do you cook or clean?

- What are your top two pet peeves?

- What are your hobbies?

- _____

- _____

- _____

- _____

- _____

- _____

- _____

Assets and Improvement

Finding and setting goals for personal improvement can seem like a daunting task. When trying to define a goal, it is equally important to reflect on your assets (strengths) and the areas in which you would like to improve. You can often use your assets to support you as you learn and set goals for a stronger you.

First identify some of your assets or strengths by listing five words that describe you.

1. _____

2. _____

3. _____

4. _____

5. _____

Now list all your assets for each of the categories here, as well as the areas in which you can grow or improve.

	Assets	Areas for Improvement
Personal life (e.g., ability to stay organized, prioritize needs, take care of physical health, practice self-care)		
Relationships (e.g., ability to maintain friendships, interact with colleagues, solve conflicts, show empathy)		
Work or school (e.g., ability to accept feedback, communicate clearly, work with others, meet deadlines)		
Other:		

Goal Builder

Answer these questions to set a clear path forward toward building obtainable personal goals. Whether it's a short-term goal that you can achieve quickly or a long-term goal that may take a while, being specific and detailed about your desired outcomes can help you define what you need to be successful and stay on track.

What do you want to achieve? Be as specific as possible.

For example: I want to obtain a job or internship. I want to drink 8 glasses of water a day. I want to be able to present in front of a large room of colleagues with confidence.

What knowledge, skills, or strategies do you currently have that will help with this goal?

What knowledge, skills, or strategies will you need?

How much time will you need to reach your goal?

What supports might you need (e.g., people, resources)?

How can you hold yourself accountable (e.g., weekly checklists, consulting with a trusted person, logging information in a calendar)?

How will you measure your goal?

On a scale of 1 to 5, how ready are you to commit to working toward your goal?

1 (Not yet)   2 (Maybe)   3 (Sure, but I may need help)   4 (Stoked!)   5 (Totally committed!)

Mini Goals

Achieving goals takes hard work and practice. To build your confidence in goal setting, try setting mini goals, which are short-term goals that are important but that you can achieve relatively quickly. First, create a daily mini goal, like "I will get to work on time." Next, outline the steps you need to be successful, such as "Set my alarm 15 minutes earlier" and "Have my work bag ready before I go to bed." Then chart your progress. Note how many times each week you are able to attain your goal. With practice, daily goals like this become routine and give way to larger goals.

Mini goal #1: _____

_____

Steps for success:

1. _____

2. _____

3. _____

Did I achieve my goal?

	Day 1	Day 2	Day 3	Day 4	Day 5	Day 6	Day 7
Yes							
No							

Mini goal #2: _____

_____

Steps for success:

1. _____

2. _____

3. _____

Did I achieve my goal?

	Day 1	Day 2	Day 3	Day 4	Day 5	Day 6	Day 7
Yes							
No							

Be a SMART Goal Setter

In-Session Exercise

When you set a goal, it is important to make sure your goal is SMART, meaning it's Specific, Measurable, Attainable, Relevant, and Time-limited. Here are the steps involved in creating a SMART goal.

- **Specific:** Create a clear, concise, and detailed goal.
- **Measurable:** Define how will you measure your success.
- **Attainable:** Select goals that are challenging but within reach.
- **Relevant:** Make sure your goal is important to you!
- **Time-limited:** Create a realistic time frame for completing your goal.

Pick one goal you noted in the Goal Builder exercise, and turn it into a SMART goal.

Specific • What do you want to accomplish? • Who or what is involved in this goal?	
Measurable • How will you measure your progress? • How will you know when you've been successful?	
Attainable • Do you have the resources to achieve this goal? • Is this a realistic goal?	
Relevant • Is this a worthwhile goal? • Does this goal align with your values?	
Time limited • What is your timeline for achieving this goal? • Can you accomplish this goal by this date?	

Success Reminders

How will you feel when you accomplish your goal? _____

Who can support you on your journey? _____

When will you reach your goal? _____

Select a midpoint date to check in and adjust as needed: _____

Weekly Accountability

Staying on track and accountable is critical if you want to reach your goals, try new tools, or change habits. Use this accountability tool to help you track your progress and recognize your daily efforts each week. First, identify a goal you'd like to track each week. For instance, perhaps your goal is to pack a lunch for work each day in order to save money. Write that goal in the "weekly goal" section, and then check off each day that you follow your plan. But don't worry if you miss a day! Instead, reflect on why you weren't able to meet your goal that day and what you might need to change so you can be successful.

Weekly goal:

Day 1	Day 2	Day 3	Day 4	Day 5	Day 6	Day 7

Weekly goal:

Day 1	Day 2	Day 3	Day 4	Day 5	Day 6	Day 7

Weekly goal:

Day 1	Day 2	Day 3	Day 4	Day 5	Day 6	Day 7

Weekly goal:

Day 1	Day 2	Day 3	Day 4	Day 5	Day 6	Day 7

Monthly Accountability

Staying on track and accountable is critical in reaching your goals. Use this accountability tool to help you track your progress and recognize your daily efforts each month. Write your goal for the month, and check off each day that you successfully work toward your goal.

Monthly goal:

1	2	3	4	5	6	7	8	9	10	11	12	13	14	15	16

Let's go! *Nice work!* *Keep going!*

17	18	19	20	21	22	23	24	25	26	27	28	29	30	31

Amazing job! *You've got this!* *Awesome job!*

Yearly Accountability

Staying on track and accountable is critical in reaching your goals. Use this accountability tool to help you track your progress and recognize your monthly efforts across the year. Write your goal for the year, and check off each month that you successfully work toward your goal.

Yearly goal:

Month 1	Month 2	Month 3	Month 4	Month 5	Month 6

Let's go! · *Nice work!* · *Keep going!*

Month 7	Month 8	Month 9	Month 10	Month 11	Month 12

Hard work pays off! · *Almost there!* · *You crushed it!*

Achieved! Goal Reflection

Bravo! You achieved your goal, so now it's time to reflect on your efforts. Reflection is a powerful tool that allows you to acknowledge the hard work you've done. Write down the goal you worked toward and why it was important to you. Then describe how it felt to accomplish this goal, any positive thoughts you have about your ability to achieve other goals, and future actions you will take given your recent success.

My goal: _____

_____

This goal was important to me because _____

_____

_____.

I feel _____ about achieving my goal.

By achieving my goal, I know that I am _____

_____.

Next time, I will (or would like to) _____

_____.

Anxiety

Young adults face many stressors as they navigate their way to independence and establish their own identity. Relationships, social media, current events, work or school responsibilities, and the pressure to achieve financial independence are all incredibly stressful. Some level of worry or anxiety is good, as it drives us to tackle hard things and put our best foot forward. However, when worry becomes unmanageable, it can interfere with our ability to eat, sleep, and think, and it can prevent us from taking healthy risks.

The activities in this chapter will help clients examine the physical and mental symptoms of anxiety and learn coping skills to better control their worries. They will also learn cognitive reframing tools to recognize faulty thinking patterns and reduce self-blame, as well as resiliency building tools to boost their social confidence and improve their ability to exert control and set limits. Finally, the mindful learning activities provide them with strategies to stay grounded while taking steps to make stress more manageable.

Getting Acquainted: Calm and Worry

Working with your clinician, answer these questions to develop a personal understanding of what it's like to feel calm versus worried.

1. Write down three words that describe *calm* to you.

   _____   _____   _____

2. Describe a recent situation where you were calm, comfortable, and confident.

   • Where did it take place? _____

   • What happened? _____

   • Who was there? _____

   • How did this make you feel? _____

   • How did your body feel? _____

3. Write down three words that describe *worry* to you.

   _____   _____   _____

4, Describe a recent situation where you were worried, uncomfortable, and anxious.

   • Where did it take place? _____

   • What happened? _____

   • Who was there? _____

   • How did this make you feel? _____

   • How did your body feel? _____

5. How often do you feel calm and in control during the week?

   Not at all   *Sometimes*   *Often*   *Most of the time*   *All the time*

6. How often do you feel nervous or uneasy during the week?

    Not at all   *Sometimes*   *Often*   *Most of the time*   *All the time*

7. List three strategies that help you feel calm in uneasy situations.

- _____

- _____

- _____

Energy Connections

Your feelings, thoughts, and body sensations are all connected. That means whenever your mood elevates or lowers, your self-talk and your physical responses shift as well. *Self-talk* refers to the way you talk to yourself, and this can range from motivating thoughts that keep you going to discouraging thoughts that interfere with your ability to get started or finish a task. Your *physical responses* include the way your body physiologically reacts (in terms of breathing, heart rate, etc.), as well as your eating habits, sleeping patterns, and overall strength. In this activity, compare how your self-talk and your physical responses differ across three different scenarios: high energy, calm energy, and low energy.

High-Energy Feelings

Examples: enthusiastic, angry, elated, excited

Self-talk: _____

_____

Physical responses: _____

_____

When are you most likely to feel this way?

What tools help your body and mind feel calm?

Calm-Energy Feelings

Examples: happy, relaxed, peaceful, focused

Self-talk: _____

_____

Physical responses: _____

_____

Low-Energy Feelings

Examples: sad, melancholy, lonely, discouraged

Self-talk: _____

_____

Physical responses: _____

_____

Whom can you turn to for support?

Worry Pyramid

Stressful situations can come in a range of intensities. In certain stressful situations, you may still feel calm and in control, whereas in others, you may feel uncomfortable or even afraid. Use this hierarchy to define the range of stressful situations that cause you to experience worry. At the base of the pyramid (1), list any stressful activities that you feel most comfortable handling. Then move up the pyramid and add examples of stressful situations where your worry intensifies. At the top of the pyramid (5), list activities that cause the highest level of worry.

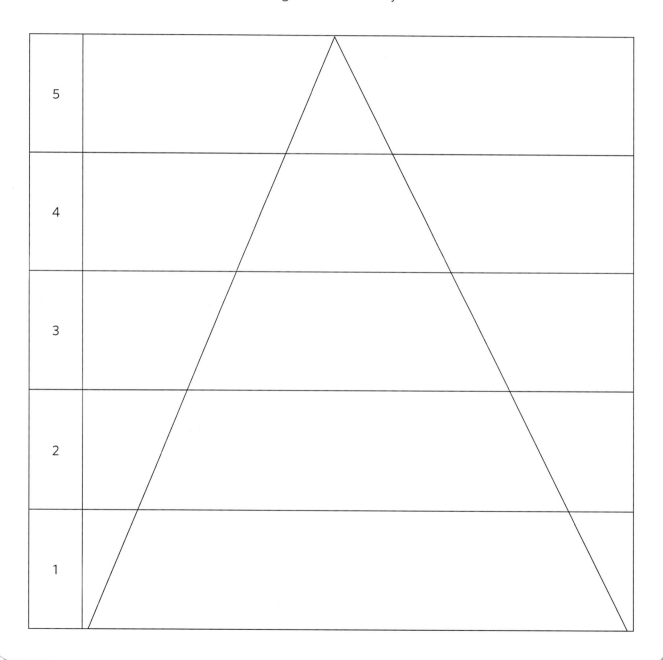

Worry Levels and Reactions

Worry comes in a range of sizes and experiences that are unique to each of us. It is important to recognize what situations increase your worry and how your body responds when this occurs. In this activity, describe different situations that make you feel varying levels of worry, and describe how your body reacts as a result (e.g., changes in breathing, sweating, movement, eating, sleeping, or concentration). Then create a short list of coping strategies that you have found to be helpful in dealing with these different levels of worry. There are no right or wrong answers to this activity. The purpose is to help you better understand your worry, how your body responds, and how you cope.

Level of Worry	Example Situation	Body Reactions	Coping Tools I Can Use When I Feel This Way
5: Extreme worry			
4: A lot of worry			
3: Some worry			
2: A little worry			
1: Very little worry			

Worry Log

Use this log to help you track events that create stress and worry. Over the next week, whenever you experience worry, write it down here. Include details about the event and what your worry was like at the time (1 = *manageable* and 5 = *totally overwhelming*). List any worrisome thoughts and how your body responded (e.g., headache, sweating, breathing changes, stomach pain). If you used any coping tools to help you feel better, include those as well. Remember that each experience is different. At the end of the week, share this information with your clinician.

Event	Level of Worry (1-5)	Worry Thoughts	Body Response	Coping Tools Used

Recognizing Faulty Thinking

Faulty thoughts are automatic judgments you have about yourself or the world that negatively cloud the way you view yourself and others. These inaccurate thoughts can create a cycle of negative feelings that interfere with your relationships, your work, and your belief in your own abilities.

Here are a few examples of faulty thinking.

Personalization: Taking everything personally and blaming yourself

"The interviewer didn't like me. That's why I didn't get the job."

Catastrophizing: Thinking something is far worse than it actually is

"My presentation was the absolute worst. I'll never get it right."

Jumping to conclusions: Making negative predictions about the future

"If I ask for help, I just know they'll say no, so why bother?"

Using one of the faulty thoughts provided (or coming up with one of your own), list some ways that this faulty thinking could impact your feelings and your actions when it comes to yourself, your relationships, and your responsibilities at work, at school, or in the community. For example, faulty thinking might have an effect on your mood, making you feel nervous or doubting your abilities. It may also have an effect on your ability to try something new or take risks at work or at school.

Faulty thought:		
Personal	**Trusted Relationships**	**Work/School/Community**
Effect on my feelings:	Effect on my feelings:	Effect on my feelings:
Effect on the actions I take:	Effect on the actions I take:	Effect on the actions I take:

Should or Could

After an argument with a friend, you might say to yourself, "I should have been more in control of my feelings!" or "I must be such a fool for getting so upset." *Should* and *must* are sneaky words that often show up when you reflect back on a challenging situation and think about what you could have done differently. These words bring up feelings of guilt or shame because they suggest that you are not living up to some rigid or unrealistic standard.

Take back control by recognizing these destructive thoughts and replacing them with a *could* statement, which is a kinder, more productive approach to self-reflection. It reminds you that while something may not have gone right the first time, there is room to grow and change. In this activity, practice shifting *shoulds* and *musts* into *coulds*.

Should or Must (Past)	Could (Future)
"I should have been more in control of my feelings."	"I could use my coping tools the next time I get upset."
"I should have passed that exam. I'll never pass this course."	
"I must not have tried hard enough. I'm such a failure."	
"I must be more in control of my fear of large groups."	
"I should have been less nervous on my date. I'll never go out again."	
"I must lose weight in order to be attractive."	

Helpful Reframe

In the scenarios that follow, you'll have a chance to practice reframing faulty thoughts with a helpful replacement thought. Your replacement thought may be positive or neutral, as long as it encourages you to take a realistic approach to a challenging situation.

1. Public speaking makes you nervous. Your boss walks into your office and asks you to lead a presentation in front of 20 colleagues.

   Unhelpful thought: *"I don't know if I can do this!"*

   Helpful reframe: *"My boss has a lot of confidence in me."*

2. It's your first week in a new apartment and you don't know anyone yet.

   Unhelpful thought: _____

   Helpful reframe: _____

3. You were in a rush and parked in the wrong spot. Now you have a parking ticket.

   Unhelpful thought: _____

   Helpful reframe: _____

4. Your credit card bill was due yesterday. You thought autopay was set up, but you discover that it was not.

   Unhelpful thought: _____

   Helpful reframe: _____

5. You made plans to go out of town with your friends this weekend. When you wake up on Friday, you are not feeling well.

   Unhelpful thought: _____

   Helpful reframe: _____

Sorting Thoughts

New transitions, like starting a new job, living on your own for the first time, or meeting new friends, can bring on a rush of thoughts that are both helpful and worrisome. Negative thoughts or intense feelings can cloud your thinking, making you focus only on what could go wrong. Use this planner to acknowledge your worries, sort those thoughts, and create a helpful action plan. First identify the transition that is headed your way. Then get your worries out of your head by writing them down. Challenge yourself to list some positive potential outcomes of the transition. Then create a positive mindset plan to encourage confidence and helpful thinking during the transition.

1. Upcoming transition:

2. I'm worried that:

3. Some positive outcomes that might happen:

4. Positive mindset plan:

When I feel: _____

I will remind myself (*positive thought*): _____

_____

Then I will feel encouraged and able to do challenging things like (*actions related to the transition*): _____

_____

Expectations of Control

You are in control of your thoughts, feelings, and actions. However, there are many situations in adulthood over which you do not have control. Knowing what you can control and what to let go of can help you better manage your expectations and stress. Next to each situation listed here, put a check mark to indicate whether you have no control, some control, or total control over the outcomes.

Situation	No Control	Some Control	Total Control
Arriving to work on time			
Whether it rains during your vacation week			
Your reaction to disappointing news			
Whether you eat healthy or unhealthy food			
Letting go of negative thoughts			
How well you prepare for a presentation or interview			
Outcome of a job interview			
Your social media posts and opinions			
Rules and restrictions at work			
How you treat others			
Keeping track of your appointments and obligations			
How you respond to feedback from a supervisor or colleague			

Self-Blame

When things go wrong, it's important to take responsibility for your role in the situation. Taking responsibility means that you hold yourself accountable—you reflect on your words and actions, apologize when appropriate, and work to solve the problem. This is different from blaming yourself—focusing on your personal insecurities, which puts the entire weight of the situation on your shoulders. In reality, there are a variety of factors that likely contributed to the unwanted outcome, some of which are in your control and some of which are out of your control.

In My Control	Out of My Control
• My actions	• Others' actions
• My feelings	• Others' feelings
• My thoughts	• Others' thoughts

Use this problem-solving worksheet to help reduce feelings of self-blame when things become challenging or don't go as planned. Write down a current situation that's causing you problems, or reflect on one from the past. Then identify the factors that you can control and those that are out of your control. Finally, brainstorm ways to solve the problem, including who can support you if needed.

Situation:

I have control over:	I do not have control over:

Next steps, solutions, and supports:

Workable Worry

Workable worries are manageable. While they may cause you some stress, you still have some control over the situation. For example, while you might be worried about how you'll perform on your upcoming driver's license exam, you are still able to study, ask for help, and try your best on the day of the test.

In contrast, unworkable worries are stressful because they concern problems that are out of your control. For example, you can't control what other people think, do, or say. You also can't control the past. Unworkable worries can negatively impact your relationships, work, and health.

With the help of a clinician, look at the two worry examples here, and mark them as workable, not workable, or possibly workable. Then add in worries that you have personally experienced and categorize those as well.

Worry	Workable	Not	Maybe?
Your friends convinced you to sign up for a 5k. You are not a runner but decide to train and try your best. The day of the race, you are worried about finishing and feel butterflies in your stomach.			
You wake up in the middle of the night, unable to sleep, worrying about whether anyone will respond to your email about a job posting.			

Guilt-Free "No"

Saying no to others can be uncomfortable, but it's an important life skill that allows you to set boundaries with others. Although it can be hard to say no when you're afraid of disappointing other people, you also risk losing your sense of self-respect if you're always putting everyone else first. Learning to speak up for your needs and choose actions based on your values is a part of the journey through adulthood.

When was the last time you said no to someone? _____

How did it make you feel? _____

What thoughts did you have at the time? _____

_____

Now let's practice. What are polite and professional ways to say no that reflect your own values and boundaries?

With friends:

When might you need to say no? _____

What might you say? _____

_____

With family members:

When might you need to say no? _____

What might you say? _____

_____

With colleagues:

When might you need to say no? _____

What might you say? _____

_____

Take Action

Learning to be independent comes with the responsibility of finding ways to problem solve during stressful moments. When stress hits, your body reacts and your mind fills with emotions that can cause you to panic rather than to problem solve. In the scenarios provided, practice helpful problem solving by describing how you could communicate your needs (*self-advocate*), use helpful thoughts to stay in control (*self-empower*), and take actions to get you through the tough situation (*self-help*).

Scenario: While checking out at the grocery store, you realize that you left your wallet at home.

Self-advocacy statement: _____

Self-empowerment thought: _____

Self-help action: _____

Scenario: While riding the bus to work, you realize that you missed your bus stop.

Self-advocacy statement: _____

Self-empowerment thought: _____

Self-help action: _____

Scenario: You make a mistake at work and become overwhelmingly nervous about how your boss will react.

Self-advocacy statement: _____

Self-empowerment thought: _____

Self-help action: _____

Create your own scenario: _____

Self-advocacy statement: _____

Self-empowerment thought: _____

Self-help action: _____

Parking Lot Thoughts

Late-night worries can ruin your rest. Whether you're worrying about a problem at work, a relationship concern, or a bill you need to pay, once you wake up, it can be hard to fall back asleep. Use this worksheet to track those late-night thoughts so you won't forget them the next day. Once you write them down, you should find it easier to fall back asleep.

Keep this form and a pen or pencil near your bed. Whenever you have a thought or worry at night, follow these steps:

1. Acknowledge your worry.

2. Remember that it can wait.

3. Write it down.

4. Address it in the morning.

Late-Night Thoughts

Are there any worries that keep coming up? Is there anything you can do during your daily routine to address them?

Parking Lot Manager

After recording your late-night worries for a while, use this worksheet to revisit those thoughts and take back control. First, read through your thoughts and identify any worries that you can manage or act upon. Write these in the table. Then, for each of these worries, list the actions you can take to help reduce your level of worry. For instance, if you wake up in the middle of the night worrying about a looming deadline for a big project, you might schedule time during the day to work on that project.

Late-Night Thought	Actions to Manage the Worry

Social Confidence Scale

Social confidence—that is, feeling comfortable in social interactions—is unique to each person and can vary by situation. There are situations in which you may be extremely comfortable and others in which you may experience significant anxiety. To better understand your levels of social confidence, write down two examples in each box that match your level of confidence in that area.

Confidence Level	My Social Examples
5: Very confident	
4: Confident	
3: Working on confidence	
2: Less confident	
1: Not at all confident!	

Social Confidence Tracker

Certain social situations can be more comfortable than others. When a social interaction is challenging, you can build confidence in your future abilities by recognizing what went well during the interaction—perhaps you overcame a worry, were assertive and advocated for yourself, or took a risk that paid off. At the end of each day, record any notable social situations that you experienced, noting what happened, where you were, and whom you were with. Rate your confidence during the interaction, using the following scale:

    1 = Not at all confident
    2 = Less confident
    3 = Working on confidence
    4 = Confident
    5 = Very confident

Also write a brief reflection on what went well. When your log is complete, share it with a trusted person or clinician.

Event	Confidence Rating (1-5)	What Went Well

Visualize Confidence

It is common for people to worry about how they'll be perceived by others. One way to overcome this worry is to imagine yourself thinking, feeling, and acting with confidence in an upcoming situation. Use this worksheet to visualize having a successful social encounter, whether you're hanging out with friends, at work, at school, or wherever else your schedule takes you.

Write down an upcoming event that is on your mind, describing in detail where it will take place, who will be there, and what will happen.

Upcoming Event	Where Is It?	Who Will Be There?	What Will Happen?

Now visualize being your best self in this situation. What emotions do you feel? What positive thoughts will you have? What actions will you take?

During the event, I will take these actions: _____

_____

During the event, I will feel _____

_____

During the event, I will have helpful thoughts like _____

_____

After the event, I will feel _____

_____

Positive Reload

Buffering isn't always about reestablishing a poor internet connection. Sometimes it's about refreshing your thoughts when negative self-talk gets you stuck in a rut. Negative self-talk can affect your feelings and prevent you from taking action, so it is important to have buffers in your life. Use this worksheet to write down positive statements that help you tackle negative thoughts and buffer, or reconnect, when times get tough.

Examples:

"I am confident and in control."

"Mistakes can help me grow."

"I've done this before. I can do it again."

↻ _____

↻ _____

↻ _____

↻ _____

↻ _____

Be Kind to Yourself

Although worries can distract you from doing your best, you can prepare for these moments by creating a weekly list of positive self-statements to help keep you centered. At the beginning of the week, write down a different encouraging statement about yourself for each day of the week. Examples of encouraging statements include, "You've got this!" or "I am capable and deserving!" Keep this worksheet nearby during the week, and if you start to feel anxious or experience self-doubt, confront those thoughts and feelings with a positive self-statement. Be kind to yourself all week long. You've got this!

Day	Positive Self-Statement
Sunday	
Monday	
Tuesday	
Wednesday	
Thursday	
Friday	
Saturday	

And the end of the week, check in with yourself. Write an example of how using these positive self-statements helped you worked through your worry.

_____

_____

_____

_____

Music Moves

Music is a powerful tool that can help you express your feelings, find a sense of calm, or release pent-up energy. What music moves you? What songs do you listen to when you want to sing at the top of your lungs, cry it out, or focus your mind? Write down these songs to create some ultimate playlists you can turn to when you want to get into a certain mood or mindset. Then create these playlists using your favorite music streaming or download service so you can access them whenever you need to. You can also share or compare your playlists with others and continue finding new songs to add and enjoy.

+ Calming Playlist

Playlist name:
_____

Songs:
_____
_____
_____
_____
_____

+ Focusing Playlist

Playlist name:
_____

Songs:
_____
_____
_____
_____
_____

+ Energizing Playlist

Playlist name:
_____

Songs:
_____
_____
_____
_____
_____

+ Motivating Playlist

Playlist name:
_____

Songs:
_____
_____
_____
_____
_____

Graceful Sailing

Imagine that you are in a sailboat at sea. If there are events that happened in the past that you wish you could change, it is common for feelings of regret, doubt, or remorse to weigh you down like an anchor, keeping you stuck in one place. To help you pull up the anchor and get unstuck, accept that these thoughts, actions, or events did occur, but don't spend much time on them. Instead, remind yourself that the past is the past, and then connect to the present moment and grant yourself grace to move forward.

To practice, take three deep breaths in and out. With each breath in, silently recite these three phrases to yourself:

I am worthy.

I am loved.

I am hopeful.

With each breath out, you fill the sail and move the boat forward.

I am worthy.

I am loved.

I am hopeful.

Gratitude Grounding

Ground yourself in gratitude. Whenever your thoughts become heavy or your feelings shift, take a moment to ground yourself in the present moment. By using the power of your five senses to connect with the present, you can cultivate a feeling of gratitude that shifts your mindset. Use the following script or make your own.

Prepare by taking three deep belly breaths in and out.

- Name five awesome things about you.

- Name four people who support you.

- Name three comfort foods you love to eat.

- Name two of your favorite songs.

- Name one thing you are grateful for.

Finish by taking three deep belly breaths in and out.

Questions to ponder:

How does this exercise make you feel?

When might these grounding questions be helpful?

How could you incorporate this into your daily routine?

Body Scan Meditation

Body scanning is a mindful practice that helps reduce tension and stress. During this activity, you'll bring awareness to your body as you tighten and release different areas of your body, starting with your feet and gradually moving up to your head. You can try this body scan as part of your relaxation routine or daily meditation practice.

1. To begin, find a comfortable place to sit or lie down.

2. Complete three guided breaths to relax. Breathe in as you count to three. Breathe out as you count to three.

3. Start by bringing awareness to your feet. Clench your toes for a count of three, then release.

4. Moving up your body, bring awareness to your legs. Squeeze your leg muscles for a count of three, then release.

5. Next, bring awareness to your midsection. Tighten the muscles in your chest and abdomen for a count of three, then release.

6. Moving outward, bring awareness to your hands. Clench your hands for a count of three, then release.

7. Moving back inward, bring awareness to your arms. Squeeze your arm muscles for a count of three, then release.

8. Finally, bring awareness to your neck, face, and head. Tighten all these muscles for a count of three, then release.

9. Finish your scan by completing three more guided breaths. Breathe in as you count to three. Then release your breath for a count of three.

CHAPTER

Depression

Moods can come and go. Some can be intense and exciting, while others can be low and tiresome, knocking us off our feet. Although it is normal for certain emotions to ebb and flow, when lower moods, like depression, take over for long periods of time, we can start to feel hopeless and isolated. These feelings of prolonged sadness or depression can cause us to withdraw from people and activities that previously brought us joy.

In this chapter, clients will find a variety of tools that will help them to identify different mood states and track them across time. A variety of cognitive reframing activities are also provided to bring awareness to automatic thoughts and distortions that can alter clients' mood, motivation, and energy levels. In addition, clients will find coping strategies they can use to develop healthy habits, find comfort, practice self-care, and connect with others. Finally, the last section contains activities to help clients shift from fixed, downward thinking to a positive, healthy mindset.

Highs and Lows Part 1:
Feeling Good

Think back to a positive experience that made you feel particularly good, elated, or excited. Then use the guiding questions here to explore what you were thinking, feeling, and doing at the time.

1. Describe a feel-good moment that you recently experienced.

What happened (event): _____

Where it took place: _____

Who was there: _____

2. During this feel-good moment, what were your thoughts, feelings, and actions?

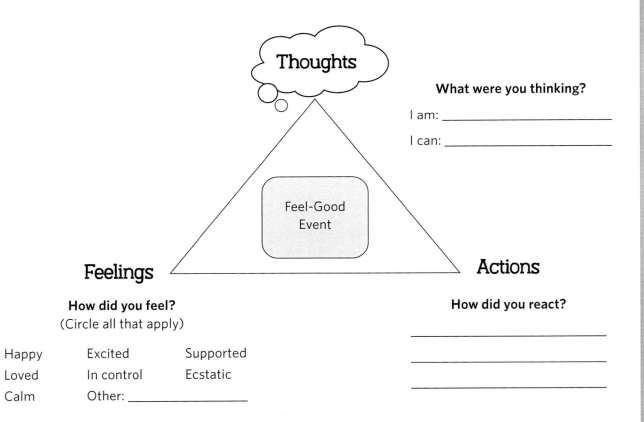

Thoughts

What were you thinking?

I am: _____

I can: _____

Feel-Good
Event

Feelings

How did you feel?
(Circle all that apply)

Happy	Excited	Supported
Loved	In control	Ecstatic
Calm	Other: _____	

Actions

How did you react?

_____

_____

_____

Highs and Lows Part 2:
Feeling Low

Think back to a time when you did not feel your best. Then use the guiding questions here to explore what you were thinking, feeling, and doing at the time.

1. Describe a recent time when you experienced a low mood.

> **What happened (event):** _____
>
> **Where it took place:** _____
>
> **Who was there:** _____

2. During this low mood, what were your thoughts, feelings, and actions?

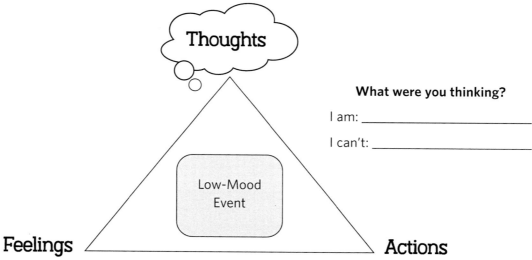

What were you thinking?

I am: _____

I can't: _____

How did you feel?
(Circle all that apply)

Upset   Disappointed   Mad

Numb   Sad   Grumpy

Other: _____

How did you react?

_____

_____

_____

Highs and Lows Part 3:
Feeling in Between

Think back to a time when you felt calm—neither very excited nor very low. Then use the guiding questions here to explore what you were thinking, feeling, and doing at the time.

1. Describe a recent time when you felt somewhere in between a high and low mood.

> **What happened (event):** _____
>
> **Where it took place:** _____
>
> **Who was there:** _____

2. During this in-between mood, what were your thoughts, feelings, and actions?

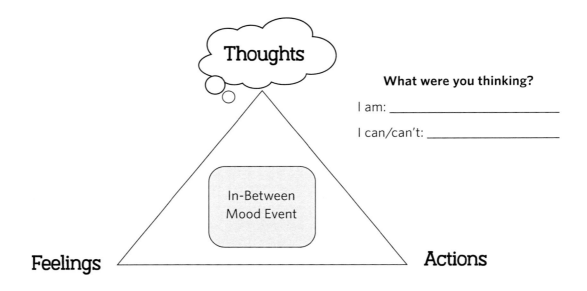

What were you thinking?

I am: _____

I can/can't: _____

In-Between Mood Event

What were you feeling?
(Circle all that apply)

Calm   Confused   Cautious
Peaceful   Indifferent   Alright
Other: _____

How did you react?

_____

_____

_____

Mood Shifts

Moods can change and adjust throughout the day, moving along a continuum. In this activity, you'll describe your personal range of moods. Start in the middle of the page by describing your calmest mood. Then describe what an elevated or excited mood is like for you, and finish by describing a depressed or low mood. Include *mental signs* (like how fast and clear your thinking is), *body signs* (like changes in muscle tension, breathing, and heart rate), and *behavior signs* (like what your activity level is like in this state). Use this worksheet as a reference to help you recognize and prepare for shifts in moods.

Elevated or Excited

Mental signs: _____

Body signs: _____

Behavior signs: _____

Calm or Relaxed

Mental signs: _____

Body signs: _____

Behavior signs: _____

Depressed or Low

Mental signs: _____

Body signs: _____

Behavior signs: _____

Daily Mood Journal

When you are sad, melancholic, or low in energy, it can seem like you *always* feel that way. But how often are you really in that mood? By tracking your moods, you can more easily identify times when you feel your best and times when you may need strategies to lift your mood or make the situation more manageable.

Use the following chart to track your daily moods for a week. At the end of each day, rate your mood for that day as a whole on a scale of 1 to 10, where 1 is "low or sad" and 10 is "happy and content." Then note any events, actions, or thoughts that influenced your daily mood. For instance, if you did well at work or made a new friend, that might have lifted your mood for the day. Or if you experienced a disappointment or had thoughts that made you second-guess yourself, your mood may have been lower.

Day	Mood Rating (1–10)	Notable Events, Actions, or Thoughts That Impacted Your Mood
Sunday		
Monday		
Tuesday		
Wednesday		
Thursday		
Friday		
Saturday		

After tracking your mood for a week or longer, what do you notice? When did you feel your best? If there were days of low mood, what strategies did you use to regroup?

_____

_____

_____

Automatic Thoughts Overview

Automatic thoughts are words or images that instantaneously (or automatically) pop into your mind in response to particular situations or life events. These pesky thinking patterns are often connected to feelings of depression or anxiety because they can negatively cloud how we perceive certain situations. They can also prevent us from taking healthy risks and from trying again when things get difficult. For instance, suppose that you recently lost contact with several friends. You need to reach out to reestablish these friendships but are reluctant to do so because you have automatic thoughts like "I'll always be lonely" or "I never have successful relationships." The truth is, these thoughts are the only thing getting in the way of your following through. Here are some guiding questions to help you approach your automatic thoughts and examine their validity.

1. On a scale of 1 to 10, how strongly do you believe this thought to be true? (With 1 being *don't believe at all* and 10 being *strongly believe*) _____

2. Has this happened before? _____

   _____

   _____

3. Is this thought helpful to yourself or others? _____

   _____

   _____

4. What evidence is there for or against this thought? _____

   _____

   _____

5. Are there any possible positive outcomes of the situation? _____

   _____

   _____

6. What might a trusted person (e.g., friend, family, clinician) say about this thought? _____

   _____

   _____

7. After going through these questions, how strongly do you believe this thought to be true now? _____

   _____

In-Session
Exercise

Exploring Distortions

Cognitive distortions are faulty or inaccurate ways of thinking that create or reinforce negative emotions. It is not uncommon to experience distortions from time to time, but they can become disruptive when they occur frequently. These types of thinking patterns can negatively affect your energy levels, focus, and motivation.

Here are a few common distortions:

- **Personalizing:** Taking things personally and seeing yourself as the cause of the problem

- **Jumping to conclusions:** Assuming you can know what someone else is thinking

- **Black-and-white thinking:** Seeing things in all-or-nothing terms with no gray zone

- **Overgeneralization:** Applying the outcome of one experience to all future experiences

- **Emotional reasoning:** Accepting your emotions as facts

- **Filtering:** Focusing only on the negatives of a situation

- **Catastrophizing:** Thinking the worst will happen

- *Should* or *must* **statements:** Imposing rules on yourself with *shoulds* or *musts*

- **Labeling:** Using negative or judgmental words to describe yourself or others

To practice identifying cognitive distortions, select a few distortions from the list and brainstorm an example that matches that type of thinking pattern.

Distortion: _____

Example: _____

_____

Distortion: _____

Example: _____

_____

Distortion: _____

Example: _____

_____

Distortion: _____

Example: _____

_____

Thought Patterns

Thoughts are connected to our feelings and actions. Helpful thoughts prepare us to tackle life challenges, keep us motivated, and help us feel safe. Less helpful (or distorted) thoughts can interfere with our day-to-day functioning by increasing feelings of worry, anxiety, or self-doubt.

Use this worksheet to gain an awareness of your daily thoughts, including the situations that triggered these thoughts. Then put a check mark to indicate whether you believe the thought is helpful or an example of a cognitive distortion. If you believe the thought is a cognitive distortion, identify the type. Share your record with your clinician to discuss patterns in your recordings.

| | | | Select One: | | |
Date	Situation	Thought	Helpful	Distortion (Include Type)	Unsure

Crush Those Automatic Thoughts

Can you recognize the difference between automatic thoughts and constructive thoughts? Test your knowledge in this activity. Crush any automatic thoughts with an X, and circle or color in any constructive thoughts. Remember: Automatic thoughts are quick judgments that negatively cloud your thinking. In contrast, constructive thoughts recognize the challenge at hand but encourage you to take a helpful and realistic approach in tackling the situation.

"Our friendship ended because I failed as a friend."

"This assignment is really difficult, so I need to practice more or ask for help."

"I'm feeling really lonely. Maybe I can call a friend tonight."

"I'm always letting others down."

"No one sees me. I'm not worth it."

"I'm not going to fit in. I am the worst at making friends. I can only trust myself."

"I'll never be happy."

"If I try something new, I might be successful."

Half-Empty or Half-Full?

It is totally valid to feel disappointed or upset when a situation does not meet your expectations. However, if you recognize a pattern where you are predicting or seeing the worst, it can skew how you perceive risks and interact with others. In this activity, practice seeing a situation from two different points of view: a glass half-empty and glass half-full. How might these views influence your actions in your personal life, at work, or at school?

Event	Half-Empty	Half-Full
You posted a picture that you really liked on social media.	"Only 13 people liked my post!"	"Wow, my friends liked the picture I shared."
You were not selected for a job that you applied for.		
You are waiting for a response from your professor after sending an email.		
You receive feedback on your work and are given an opportunity to make changes.		
Add your own situation:		

All-or-Nothing Thinking

All-or-nothing thinking is a common cognitive distortion that limits our problem-solving abilities because it causes us to see in extremes: black or white, right or wrong. The first step in recognizing this type of faulty thinking to identify the words that create divides, like *never*, *always*, *all*, or *every*. Read the statements and underline the words that indicate a divide.

Thought Tracker

In the chart, record any life events that happen over the course of the next week, making sure to describe your initial thoughts about the event as well as the actual outcomes. The purpose of tracking these is to see if your initial thought matches the outcome you predicted. By doing this, you can identify patterns of negative or automatic thinking that might be getting in your way.

Event	Initial Thoughts	Outcome
I started reading the driver's manual to prepare for my driver's license knowledge test.	I am excited but I am not sure I will ever learn all these rules.	I made a plan to study each night leading up to the test and was able to pass the test.

Reframing Practice

For this activity, write down a recent problem you encountered that was difficult to handle and that made you upset. Describe any negative thoughts that emerged about the problem, how your body felt, and the actions you took at the time. Then brainstorm what tools you could use in the future to better navigate this situation or seek help, and try problem solving again. Reframe your initial negative thought, list actions you could take to help you cope, and imagine how your body will feel when you've dealt with the problem.

Past problem: _____

Thoughts I Had	Actions I Took	How My Body Felt

Next time: _____

Helpful Thoughts I Can Tell Myself	Coping Skills I Can Use to Stay in Control	How My Body Will Feel

Future Focus

Negative thoughts and feelings can make it seem like nothing will ever go right. In those moments, looking forward to the future can help shift your mindset. Use this activity to create a reminder of positive or happy events that are coming up or wishes you have for the future. The events can be small, like a call from a loved one or a visit with a family member, or they can involve bigger plans for a special day ahead.

Tomorrow I am looking forward to:

This week I am looking forward to:

This month I am looking forward to:

This year I am looking forward to:

Turn It Up

Depression can negatively impact your self-view, energy, motivation, healthy habits, and ability to connect with others. Use this worksheet to highlight strategies you can use and supportive people you can turn to when you need a boost in one or more of the areas listed here.

↑ Self-view

My tools:	My supports:

↑ Energy

My tools:	My supports:

↑ Motivation

My tools:	My supports:

↑ Healthy habits
(e.g., eating, sleeping, exercising)

My tools:	My supports:

↑ Social connection

My tools:	My supports:

↑ Add your own:
_____

My tools:	My supports:

Worst Day Rewind

Describe a recent situation that just didn't go your way. Then rewind it and try it over again by going through these problem-solving steps:

1. Recognize your feelings.

2. Pause and let your feelings settle.

3. Brainstorm solutions and outcomes.

4. Determine your plan of action.

While you may have to accept the initial outcome of the situation, you will be prepared to handle the next challenge ahead.

Describe the situation: _____

_____

_____

Recognize: How did this make you feel? _____

_____

_____

Pause: Let your feelings settle.

Brainstorm solutions:

Possible solution 1: _____

Possible solution 2: _____

Determine your plan of action: _____

_____

_____

Meal Tracker

How does stress alter your eating habits? Perhaps it causes you to you eat too much, to eat comfort food instead of healthy food, or to skip meals altogether. Use this meal tracker to gain insight on your eating patterns and how they're connected to your stress levels.

Over the next week, jot down every time you eat a meal or snack, making sure to note the date and time. Then rate your stress level at the time using a 5-point scale, with 1 being *very calm* and 5 being *totally stressed out*. Finally, describe any notable events that were occurring at the time. Sometimes big events, like giving a presentation at work, temporarily alter our eating habits. Be honest when filling out the form, as this information will help identify potential habits or patterns when it comes to your eating behavior.

Date	Time	What You Ate	Stress Level (1–5)	Notable Events

Get Up and Move

Exercise is a great way to relieve stress and to increase your body's natural mood boosters, which are called endorphins. Increase positive feelings by making exercise a priority today. Different days may call for different kinds of movement, so use this list to brainstorm the types of exercise that help you stay calm, manage stress, gain focus, or increase energy. Then make a plan to add movement into your weekly schedule.

Purpose	Type of Movement or Exercise
Stay calm	
Manage stress	
Gain focus	
Feel energized	

What will you try this week?

Sunday	
Monday	
Tuesday	
Wednesday	
Thursday	
Friday	
Saturday	

Connection Plan

Staying connected with family, friends, and colleagues is an important part of buffering yourself against the effects of depression and social isolation. List all your important connections in the circle. Then create a connection plan to remind you of ways to connect with the people in your life who love and support you.

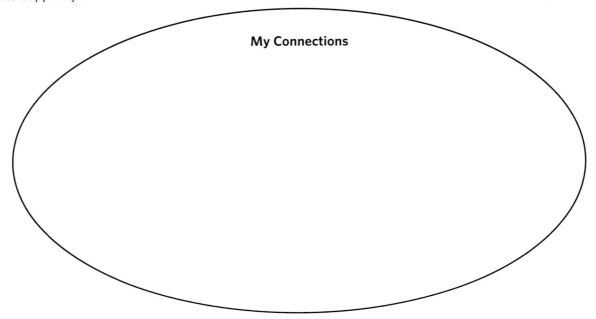

My Connections

I can connect with family by _____

_____

I can connect with friends by _____

_____

I can connect with colleagues by _____

_____

Get Your Rest

Restful sleep allows the body to relax and recharge. Most adults require seven to nine hours of sleep a night. How much sleep are you running on? Review the sleep tips here, and then create your own sleep routine to promote restful, helpful sleep.

Sleep Tips

- What time do you need to wake up? Rewind seven to nine hours. That is your new bedtime!

- Identify what you need to relax. Quiet, calming music? White noise? Low light?

- Set a curfew for electronics about an hour before you want to be asleep.

- Select an activity to help calm your mind before bed (e.g., reading, listening to music, meditating).

My Sleep Routine

Positive Affirmations

Positive affirmations are sayings that remind you of what you can control, that affirm your worth, that acknowledge your efforts, and that allow you to grant yourself some grace. Review the list of affirmations provided here, and then come up with three that are most meaningful to you. You can select from the list here or write your own. Then read your affirmations each day and remember: You've got this!

- I am STRONG.

- I am connected.

- My life has meaning and value.

- I try to see the best in others.

- I am worthy of happiness.

- I am proud of my accomplishments.

- I am worthy of love.

- I choose happiness.

- I am capable.

- I am resilient.

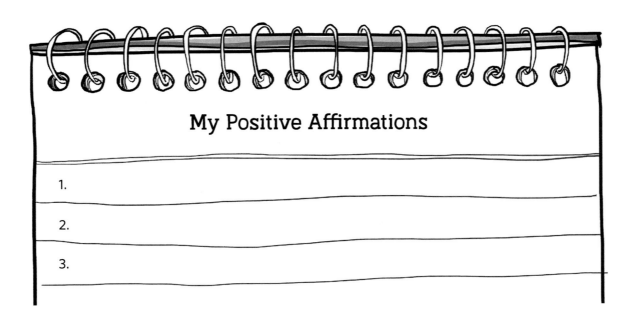

My Positive Affirmations

1.

2.

3.

10-Day Positivity Challenge

Take the 10-day positivity challenge. Purposely engage in three positive actions each day that support your body, mind, and connection to others. Fill in the chart as you complete each task. If 10 days seems too easy, try it for 30 days!

1. **Healthy habits:** Nourish your body with healthy meals, make sleep a priority, and take time to exercise.

2. **Positive affirmations:** Say three positive affirmations each day, noting your efforts and the gifts you bring to the world.

3. **Connection to others:** Intentionally reach out to loved ones and friends by writing a letter, calling, texting, and so on.

	Healthy Habits	Positive Affirmations	Connection to Others
Day 1			
Day 2			
Day 3			
Day 4			
Day 5			
Day 6			
Day 7			
Day 8			
Day 9			
Day 10			

Soothe Your Soul

Use your senses to explore the sights, sounds, feelings, tastes, and smells that bring you comfort. Write down a few of your favorite sensory experiences under each heading, such as the smell of lavender or the sound of rain. Use this tool as a guide to integrate sensory experiences into your self-care routine, surrounding yourself with experiences that soothe your soul.

Feelings

Sounds

Smells

_____

_____

_____

_____

_____

_____

Tastes

_____

_____

_____

Sights

_____

_____

_____

_____

_____

_____

_____

_____

Good Day Diary

Think about a day that you really enjoyed, and write a letter to your future self about this good day. Be sure to include how you felt, what did you did, and who helped make the day so enjoyable—all the good stuff. Use this letter to remind yourself of better times when things might not be going your way. Better days are ahead, and you are worthy of being happy.

Dear Self,

Today was a good day! _____

_____

_____

_____

_____

_____

_____

_____

_____

_____

_____

_____

_____

_____

_____

Love,

_____

P.S. You are capable and awesome.

Traumatic Stress

Young adults often carry with them current or past experiences that cause significant pain or stress. These adverse or traumatic experiences can significantly reduce their trust in others, interfere with their overall well-being, and limit their sense of safety. Clinicians who treat traumatic stress are tasked with establishing trust and creating a safe space where clients can discuss these important experiences. Therefore, the focus of this section is to support clients who have experienced traumatic stress by helping them communicate their feelings and by finding ways to make those feelings more manageable.

The first set of activities in this chapter will help clients better understand the connection between difficult memories and their overall mood. The subsequent tools teach clients to recognize faulty thinking patterns and help them shift away from all-or-nothing thinking and self-blame. Resiliency activities are also included to help clients find greater safety and control, develop connections with others, and make stress more manageable. Finally, self-care activities are included to highlight clients' personal strengths, foster empowerment, and focus on building healthy habits.

Emotional Explorer

There are hundreds of ways to describe how you feel. While some emotions are more pleasant than others, all emotions are valid because they describe your personal experience.

Your emotions have both a physical component (how your body responds, such as changes in energy, muscle tension, heart rate, or breathing) and a mental component (how your mind responds, such as certain thoughts or memories). For this activity, share your personal experience with each of the emotions listed here by describing how you feel it, both physically and mentally. And be assured: All experiences are valid!

	Excited, Enthusiastic, Elated
Physical experience	
Mental experience	

	Melancholic, Distressed, Sad
Physical experience	
Mental experience	

	Nervous, Guilty, Envious
Physical experience	
Mental experience	

	Your Choice: _____
Physical experience	
Mental experience	

Memories and Experiences

Memories can bring back a variety of different feelings, ranging from comfort and joy to stress and fear. Talking about these feelings can be challenging, but it can also provide a path toward healing. Use this template to talk about your memory of two safe experiences and one difficult experience from your past.

Safe Memory

_____

_____

_____

_____

➤ Feelings: _____

_____

Relevant details (e.g., setting, people, or events): _____

_____

_____

Difficult Memory

_____

_____

_____

_____

➤ Feelings: _____

_____

Relevant details (e.g., setting, people, or events): _____

_____

_____

Safe Memory

_____

_____

_____

_____

➤ Feelings: _____

_____

Relevant details (e.g., setting, people, or events): _____

_____

_____

My Experience

Sharing a stressful or traumatic experience can be overwhelming. Even when you are with a trusted person, like a clinician, it can be challenging to recall memories or to sequence events because of the feelings and thoughts connected to the event. That's okay. When you are comfortable and ready, work with your trusted person to complete the following sentences to share your important narrative. Remember that your feelings and experiences are important, personal, and valid.

I remember when _____

_____.

First, _____

_____.

Next, I remember _____

_____.

Then _____

_____.

I remember feeling _____

_____.

I remember thinking _____

_____.

I would like to feel _____.

I feel safest when _____.

These are the people I trust and who support me: _____

_____

When I am confronted with feelings or thoughts that make me feel unsafe, I can _____

_____.

Memories and Mood

Memories or flashbacks of traumatic or stressful events can impact your mood, thoughts, and actions. They may make you feel a variety of feelings, like unsafe, startled, distracted, or overwhelmed. How often does this happen to you? Use this tracker to gain an understanding of when memories appear and how they impact your daily life. After you take note of your experiences between sessions, share your findings with your clinician. This information can help you connect your memories to your mood, allowing you to identify more effective coping tools to keep you feeling safe and in control.

Describe the Memory	What Were You Doing When the Memory or Flashback Occurred?	How Did You Feel?

Safe Feelings and Responses

The concept of safety is shaped by our personal experiences and perceptions. With the support of your clinician, describe what it means to feel safe and what it means to feel uneasy or even threatened. Describe the emotions, thoughts, and body sensations you have in response to these two different experiences. What can you do to feel secure again when you notice your feelings shift?

	Safe and Comfortable	Unsure or Threatened
What does this feeling mean to you?		
When did you feel this way?		
What kind of emotions did you feel?		
What kind of thoughts did you have?		
How did your body feel?		

What can you do when you start to feel uneasy? _____

_____

Whom can you connect with? _____

_____

What can others do to help you? _____

_____

Thoughts, Feelings, and Actions

In-Session Exercise

Our thoughts, feelings, and behaviors are all connected, so a life event that changes our thinking patterns will also change the way we feel and act. For example, positive or encouraging events promote healthy feelings, positive thinking, and helpful actions. On the other hand, discouraging, stressful, and possibly traumatic events can negatively skew our mindset. Use this worksheet to identify two positive events and two stressful events that you have encountered in your life, including what you were thinking at the time of the event, what emotions you were feeling, and how these two factors influenced the actions you took.

Event	Thoughts	Feelings	Actions
Encouraging or positive event:			
Encouraging or positive event:			
Discouraging or stressful event:			
Discouraging or stressful event:			

Shaping Thoughts and Feelings

Painful experiences can negatively shape the way we think about ourselves and cause us to feel frustrated, angry, confused, or even ashamed. Although we often take these negative thoughts at face value, they are usually not true. In this activity, you'll have an opportunity to practice replacing negative thoughts with more helpful thoughts that foster positive feelings. To do so, first check for evidence for or against the negative thought, and then find a replacement thought that provides you with more encouragement. An example is provided for you first, followed by some space for you to fill in your own.

Current Thought	Current Feeling	Is the Negative Thought True? (Provide Evidence)
I will never find someone who loves me.	Discouraged, sad, alone	It's not true because there are plenty of people in my life who love me and care about me. Just because I had a painful breakup doesn't mean that I won't find someone else who values me the way my friends and family do.
Replacement Thought	**Replacement Feeling**	
I am worthy. I am loved. I am capable.	Confident, excited, relieved, supported	

Current Thought	Current Feeling	Is the Negative Thought True? (Provide Evidence)
Replacement Thought	**Replacement Feeling**	

Bad News Filter

Listening to bad news can be overwhelming and even blinding at times. The same is true with self-talk, which functions like your inner news feed. For instance, let's say you made a major mistake at work. Although everyone makes mistakes, you are embarrassed and upset. Your negative thoughts take over—like "I'm not a good person" or "I'll never do anything right"—which can really derail your progress. Whenever you find yourself listening to "bad news" or negative self-talk, try counterbalancing it with constructive action to help shift your feelings:

1. Recognize your efforts, including the time and work you put into doing something, even if the outcome was not what you were hoping.

2. Take a minute to connect with the present moment by doing a mindfulness activity, like meditating, deep breathing, or coloring.

3. Engage in a self-care practice, like connecting with those who lift you up or taking "me" time.

Use the chart to record any instances when you experience negative self-talk. Then decide what constructive action you can take to move forward.

Negative Self-Talk	Constructive Action

Partly Cloudy

Life is full of learning opportunities and mistakes. After you make a mistake, it's easy to approach the situation with a cloudy view and to tell yourself, "I'm not good enough." Although you might not have mastered whatever it is you tried to do, that does not define your ability. Instead, look at how you might be able to learn and grow from the experience by reframing the situation: "I may not be good enough *yet*." In this activity, acknowledge a time when you did not think you were good enough. Then reframe your thought with a sunnier view.

Breathe and Remember:

I'm still learning.

I'm getting better.

I'll keep trying.

Cloudy View

"I wasn't selected for the committee. I'm not good enough for it anyway."

Sunnier View

"I didn't get selected *yet*. I just need a bit more experience."

Neutral Zone

Describe your neutral zone: the place where you feel safe, calm, and in control. In this neutral zone, you can adjust to your surroundings, problem solve, and do your best. When life gets stressful and you move out of your comfort zone, what strategies help bring you back? Use this activity to guide this discussion. Describe your neutral zone in words or pictures, including what the surroundings are like, who is around you, and how you feel. Then write down five ways to shift back into neutral after a stressful situation or day.

My Neutral Zone

P
R
N
D
2
1

Five Ways to Shift into Neutral

1. _____

2. _____

3. _____

4. _____

5. _____

In-Session
Exercise

Stress Continuum

Stress comes in many different shapes and sizes. Use this scale to gain a better understanding of what makes you feel calm and in control and what causes stress to become less manageable. Describe activities, tasks, places, or locations associated with different kinds of stress. Then describe coping skills you can use to manage these different levels of stress.

Stress Level	Tasks or Activities	Places or Locations
5: Extremely stressed		
4: Very stressed		
3: Uncomfortable		
2: A little anxious		
1: No stress; calm and in control		

What coping strategies help when you are in the 2–3 range? _____

_____

_____

What coping strategies help when you are in the 4–5 range? _____

_____

_____

Stress and Me Recorder

After you complete the Stress Continuum exercise, use this chart to continue gaining greater awareness of the daily experiences that evoke stress, as well as those that make you feel calm and in control. Over the next week, keep track of any notable events that occur, making sure to include information on who was there, what the event involved, and where it took place. If the event was associated with stress, describe any coping skills you used to help manage the situation.

Date	Event	Stress Rating (1-5)	Coping Tools

Fight, Flight, Freeze, and Calm Feelings

When you're confronted with a challenging or stressful situation, your body and mind respond by activating the fight, flight, and freeze response. Use this exercise to reflect on how you feel in each of these states. Start by creating a baseline of how your body and mind handle situations when you are calm and cool. Then describe what your body and mind have felt like in past situations where you wanted to lash out (fight), had the urge to escape or run away (flight), or felt stuck in your tracks (freeze).

	Calm and Cool	Fight	Flight	Freeze
Muscles (e.g., tense, relaxed, shaky)				
Concentration (e.g., focused, distracted, alert)				
Communication (e.g., quick, clear, confusing)				
Breathing (e.g., rapid, shallow, deep)				
Digestion (e.g., stomach cramps, nausea, indigestion)				
Body temperature (e.g., sweaty, cool, cold, hot)				
Feelings (e.g., relaxed, on edge, anxious, happy)				
Interactions with others				
Actions				
Other				

Coping Strategies for Stressful Feelings

How do you cope with situations that make you want to fight, flee, or freeze? There are many ways to constructively manage this range of stress responses. Use this chart to build a list of coping tools you can use across each situation, taking note of strategies and other forms of support that can help you defuse difficult feelings. Add to this list as you learn new strategies that you find useful.

When I Want to Escape...	
What can I do?	
What do I need?	
How can others help me?	
When I Want to Fight...	
What can I do?	
What do I need?	
How can others help me?	
When I Am Frozen...	
What can I do?	
What do I need?	
How can others help me?	

Stressful Reflection

Stress and anxiety are the body's way of protecting you from perceived threats. At times, though, the mind interprets an event as threatening when it's really a false alarm. Although false alarms are normal—since stress is an unavoidable part of life—too many false alarms can keep you on edge and interfere with your daily life. Use this reflection tool to think about the day-to-day events that cause you stress, taking note of any associated thoughts, feelings, physical symptoms, and behaviors you have in response to these triggers. Rate the level of stress you felt (with 1 being *very low stress* and 5 being *high stress*), and note whether the situation was a real alarm or a false alarm. You can either complete this activity in session or use it as a homework tool to discuss your experiences between sessions.

Event (setting, details):	**Stress response** (e.g., physical symptoms, feelings, thoughts, actions):
Stress level: 1 2 3 4 5	☐ Real alarm ☐ False alarm ☐ Not sure

Event (setting, details):	**Stress response** (e.g., physical symptoms, feelings, thoughts, actions):
Stress level: 1 2 3 4 5	☐ Real alarm ☐ False alarm ☐ Not sure

Event (setting, details):	**Stress response** (e.g., physical symptoms, feelings, thoughts, actions):
Stress level: 1 2 3 4 5	☐ Real alarm ☐ False alarm ☐ Not sure

Wave Rider

Intense feelings can be compared to a wave. As the wave comes closer to shore, it builds energy, crests, and then releases. We may not know when that wave is coming, but we can prepare for when it does arrive. What tools can you use to help you stay safe and ride the wave? Answer the questions here to help you visualize how you might prepare yourself when those feelings start building in intensity.

Think of a previous time when you rode an emotion wave. What was the situation or event that triggered these intense feelings? _____

_____

When your emotions run high, how long do these feelings typically last? _____

_____

Describe your safe space when emotions run high. _____

_____

During this time, what do you need the most? _____

_____

During this time, what do you *not* want? _____

_____

The next time an emotion wave comes ashore and you need help, what can you do? _____

_____

After the wave passes, how can you reflect on the experience (e.g., journaling, sharing with your clinician or a family member)? _____

_____

Feeling and Being

You are worthy and loved, but when life becomes overwhelming, it can be hard to feel this way. In this activity, you'll have an opportunity to engage in a creative practice that will help you calm your body, connect to the present, and shift your thoughts to a more peaceful state. To get your creativity flowing, first describe what it means to feel safe.

Where do you feel safe? _____

_____

What makes you feel safe? _____

_____

Who makes you feel safe? _____

_____

Now, using the space provided or a separate sheet of paper, create an image that represents safety to you. This image can be one that you draw yourself, or you can cut and paste images that you find online or in magazines. Display your work of art in a visible location so you can use it during challenging times to remind yourself of your connection and safety.

Love, Me

After a painful, stressful, or disempowering experience, you can sometimes lose your sense of self. When this happens, it's important to remind yourself of your personal strengths—of all the positive traits you bring to the world. Use this activity to write down all the amazing, wonderful qualities that make you special. Fill these spaces with love. When you're done, reflect on what you've written, and give gratitude to your body and mind for all that they do.

Fill Your Bucket

What activities fill your joy bucket? Finding room for activities in your busy day is an important part of taking care of yourself. Look at the self-care ideas here and brainstorm any others you'd like to try. What activities speak to you? What others can you add to your self-care routine?

Acts of Service	Me Time
• Volunteer • Mentor or tutor someone • Perform an act of kindness	• Relax in any way you choose • Laugh • Prioritize exercise and movement
Healthy Boundaries	**Exploring Your Creative Self**
• Set boundaries (e.g., say no to others) • Connect with supportive people (e.g., family, friends, support groups) • Set limits with social media, emails, or phone calls	• Take a painting, photography, or cooking class • Listen to new or soothing music, or create your own • Try a DIY project or a new recipe

List all the self-care ideas you'd like to try to fill your bucket:

Acts of Service	Me Time
Healthy Boundaries	**Exploring Your Creative Self**
Other Ideas	

Shield of Self-Belief

Believe in yourself and your abilities to try, persist, and overcome challenges. Write down five
affirmations (or positive phrases) that can help you defeat self-doubt and stay true to your goals and
dreams.

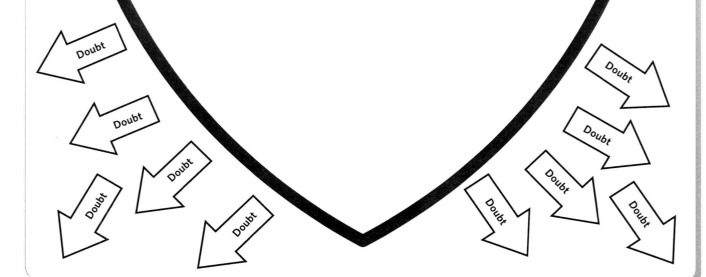

Positive Affirmations

1. _____

2. _____

3 . _____

4. _____

5. _____

10 Mindful Steps

As you travel on your journey to becoming a successful, independent adult, grant yourself some grace as you take each step. Create a list of 10 encouraging words to help strengthen your bridge and take you into the future. Consider reciting these words of encouragement on a walk or when you need a moment to yourself. You deserve it!

Step 1. _____

Breathe

Step 2. _____

Breathe

Step 3. _____

Breathe

Step 4. _____

Breathe

Step 5. _____

Breathe

Step 6. _____

Breathe

Step 7. _____

Breathe

Step 8. _____

Breathe

Step 9. _____

Breathe

Step 10. _____

Attention-Deficit/Hyperactivity Disorder

Although attention-deficit/hyperactivity disorder (ADHD) is diagnosed most often in childhood, the disorder can continue to impact clients well into adulthood. The inattention and impulsivity symptoms that accompany ADHD can negatively affect clients' self-esteem, relationships, and executive function skills, which are imperative for success in adulthood.

The first set of activities in this chapter will help increase clients' understanding of their ADHD symptoms, particularly in terms of their distractibility and restlessness. Positive reframing activities then shift the focus from perceived deficits to strengths and teach clients how to advocate for their needs. In addition, resiliency activities highlight strategies clients can use to strengthen their problem-solving abilities, manage their emotions, and build executive function skills that promote time management and other helpful work habits. Finally, the section on mindful organization offers ways clients can create a focused workspace and develop organized routines.

Focused and Distracted

Focused: What does it mean to be focused and attentive? What does it look like to you? Consider all the settings in which you must be focused and the different demands you face in each. During which events, activities, or times of the day are you at your best? List your strengths in each setting.

At Home	At School or Work	With Others

Distracted: Being unable to concentrate can impact people in different ways. It can affect their relationships with others, their work performance, and their ability to follow through with daily tasks (e.g., paying bills on time, organizing important information, cleaning). Reflect on the ways inattention has impacted you in each of these settings. When and where does being inattentive impact your performance the most?

At Home	At School or Work	With Others

Quick Thinking and Impulsivity

Quick thinking: The ability to make quick decisions or act on the fly can be beneficial in certain settings. In each of the areas listed here, note any events, activities, or times of the day when your quick decision-making comes in handy.

At Home	At School or Work	With Others

Impulsivity: Acting impulsively can also have its drawbacks in certain settings. How does acting impulsively negatively affect you in each of these settings? When and where does impulsivity impact your performance the most?

At Home	At School or Work	With Others

Inattention Tracker

Use this worksheet to track times when you experience inattention or loss of focus. When you find yourself finding it difficult to start daily tasks, having trouble sustaining focus, or even forgetting about tasks, write it down. Think about what's going on, what needs to be done, and how you are feeling. Track these thoughts for a week. Share your findings with your clinician to see if any patterns emerge so you can find strategies to support you in times of inattention.

First define how you experience inattention. What does it look and feel like?

_____

_____

_____

Then keep track of your inattention throughout the week.

Date/ Time	What Was Going On?	What Did I Miss?	Coping Tools Used

Restlessness Tracker

Use this worksheet to track times when you feel restless. When you find yourself overly distracted or irritable, or have trouble staying in one place, write it down. Think about what's going on, what needs to be done, and how you are feeling. Track these thoughts for a week. Share your findings with your clinician to see if any patterns emerge so you can find strategies to help you cope with restlessness.

First define how you experience restlessness. What does it look and feel like?

_____

_____

_____

Then keep track of your restlessness through the week.

Date/Time	What Was Going On?	What Did I Miss?	Coping Tools Used

Focused on Strength: Defining Strengths

This activity is designed to help you recognize areas of strength that may set you apart from others. This can help shift your perspective from "I can't" to "I can" when it comes to your ADHD symptoms. What makes you unique and powerful? Reflect on your best days, and write down your skills in each of the areas listed. Some example ideas are provided below.

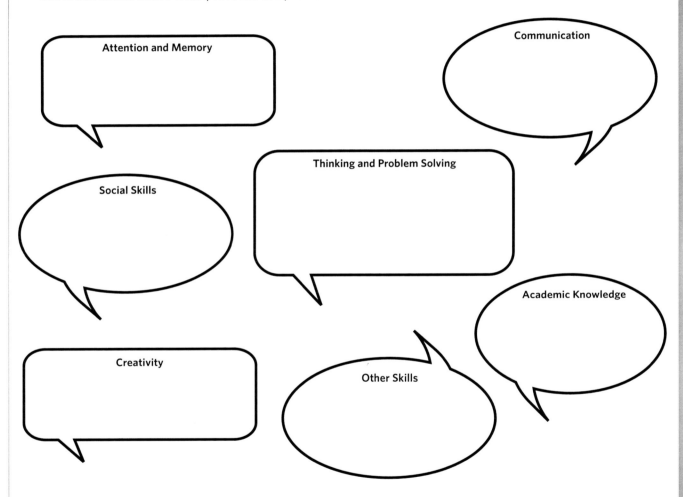

Attention and Memory

Communication

Thinking and Problem Solving

Social Skills

Academic Knowledge

Creativity

Other Skills

Thinking and Problem Solving
- Creative
- Focused
- Attentive to detail
- Goal focused
- Problem solver

Social Skills
- Empathic
- Collaborative
- Friendly
- Outgoing
- Engaging

Communication
- Able to relate to others
- Expressive
- Clear and concise
- Articulate
- Perspective taker

Focused on Strength: Supporting Strengths

This activity is designed to help you identify elements in your environment or accommodations that you have found helpful in supporting your personal strengths. As you get older, it is key to recognize strategies that help you present your most successful self. In each of the areas listed, write down strategies, previous accommodations, or tools that you have found useful in supporting you. Some suggestions for helpful tools are provided below.

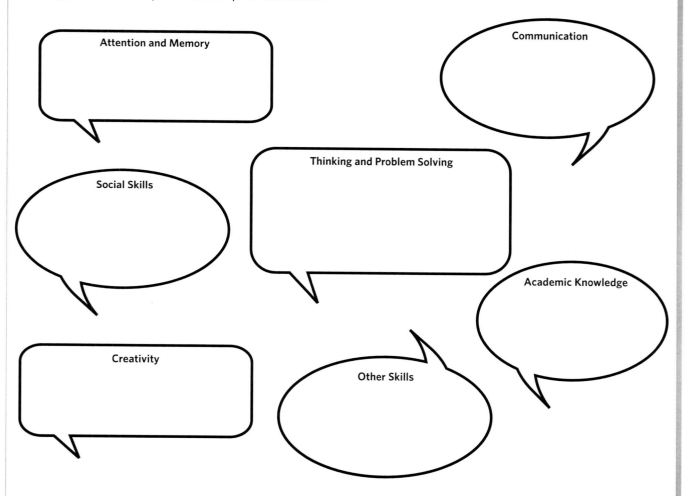

Thinking and Problem Solving
- Asking clarifying questions
- Setting goals
- Brainstorming
- Using visual aids

Social Skills/Communication
- Remembering others' feelings
- Setting boundaries
- Engaging with others
- Reviewing expectations of different settings

Attention and Memory
- Using calendars
- Setting time limits
- Finding a quiet place to work
- Chunking large projects

Positive Altitudes

When negative automatic thoughts invade your mental space, lift your attitude with three positive thoughts. In the spaces provided, write down any troublesome negative thoughts. Then leave those negative thoughts behind by filling up each hot air balloon with three positive statements about yourself. Remember: There are many wonderful things about you!

Example:

	Positive Thoughts
	I will try my best.
Negative Thought	I can do it.
My presentation will be a failure!	I've done all I can to prepare.

Cheer Me On!

Be your own cheerleader! Celebrate your successes because you should be proud of your progress. Write down a list of all your accomplishments, including any major wins (like getting a promotion at work) or minor wins (like completing a list of daily errands). Whatever it is, write down at least one accomplishment a day, and watch your victories pile up. After you make a running list, take time to reflect on your hard work.

My Victories

Post It, Hold It, or Delete It

Social media is a helpful medium to connect with others and share ideas. However, posting on these platforms requires responsibility and an understanding of how your responses may have consequences. Review the following actions, and discuss whether you should post it, hold onto it while you decide if it's a good idea, or just delete it.

	Post It	Hold It	Delete It
Post a funny picture of your pet			
Share your feelings about a situation at your workplace			
Share an accomplishment, such as getting a promotion or completing a program			
Post a "happy birthday" message to a friend			
Talk about a controversial meme that you find funny			
Respond with strong disagreement to a post shared by a friend or family member			
Share every detail of your weekend, from mundane tasks to going out at night			
Post a picture of yourself and your friends at a party			
Share a positive review of a new restaurant			
Add your own:			
Add your own:			
Add your own:			
Add your own:			

Thinking It Through

When a problem or crisis arises, your feelings surge and it's easy to act without thinking. Although acting on your feelings can sometimes protect you from danger or provide you with quick relief, it can also result in impulsive decision-making that has other consequences.

Identify a recent time when you acted on your feelings and perhaps acted impulsively (e.g., jumped to conclusions, blurted something out in a meeting). Then imagine replaying that situation. Take a deep breath and think of two other ways you could have handled the problem. How would you have responded differently? And how might others have reacted to these new outcomes?

Situation: _____

_____

	Acted on Feelings (It happens!)
What did you say?	
How did you act?	
How did you feel?	
How did others react?	

Situation Redo

	Solution # 1	Solution #2
What would you say?		
How would you act?		
How might you feel?		
How might others react?		

Self-Monitoring Intervals

Self-monitoring is a strategy to bring awareness to how often you engage in certain behaviors. This technique is helpful if you want to increase your productivity or improve your active listening skills. It may also help decrease behaviors that are interfering with your success, like checking social media or roaming around to avoid doing work.

For this task, indicate what behavior you want to monitor, and define what it looks like to you. This will be your target behavior. Then select a time frame and a time interval during which you'd like to monitor how frequently you engage in this behavior. Set a timer to alert you at each interval. When the timer goes off, indicate whether you are engaging in the target behavior. When time ends, review your progress. Try this activity a few times to build success with bringing awareness to your target behavior.

Target Behavior	What It Looks Like

Select time frame (e.g., 10 minutes, 20 minutes): _____

Select time interval (e.g., every 30 seconds, 1 minute): _____

When the timer sounds, put a check mark in each box to indicate if you are engaging in the target behavior at each interval, or leave the box blank if you successfully avoided engaging in the target behavior.

Trial 1	1	2	3	4	5	6	7	8	9	10
	11	12	13	14	15	16	17	18	19	20

Trial 2	1	2	3	4	5	6	7	8	9	10
	11	12	13	14	15	16	17	18	19	20

Fidget Plan

Fidgeting can be helpful in keeping your mind moving and on task, whether it's tapping your foot, standing at your workspace, or moving a small gadget in your hand. However, fidgeting can also be disruptive, such as when you are pacing around the room, making noises with your hand, or popping gum—to name a few. It's important to gain awareness regarding your fidget habits as you get older because you may need to adjust your movements to your environment. For instance, you have more freedom to move about at home, but at work or school, you need to find ways to fidget that are not disruptive to yourself or others. Work out a plan to help you become more intentional about what fidget strategies you use.

	Home (Around Family)	Work or School (Around Colleagues)	Social (Around Friends)
Preferred fidget strategies			
When, where, and how?			

Mindful Movement Breaks

Taking a purposeful break each hour to move, stand, stretch, or go on a short walk can help keep the blood flowing and the work going. Use this activity to brainstorm how you can incorporate purposeful movement into your day so you can take a short break, refresh, and then return to work.

To begin, write down what your daily schedule looks like. Then underline activities or times of day when you are *most* focused, and star activities or times of day when you are *less* focused. Focus on the starred activities and times when rewriting schedule. What types of movement could be helpful?

Time	Activity

Next, brainstorm the types of movement that are possible during your day: _____

_____

_____

Finally, rewrite your schedule, making sure to incorporate movement breaks to help you stay on task.

Time	Activity and Movement

Remind Me

Adulting is not easy! You are responsible for keeping your personal and work life organized. To make this easier, it helps to create a few visual reminders. This is especially the case if you are adding a new routine to your schedule. Use this worksheet to create a few reminders to keep you organized, and indicate where you will put them so you see them every day.

Examples:

Location: On the front door

Leaving for Work
- ✓ Wallet
- ✓ Phone
- ✓ Keys
- ✓ Computer
- ✓ Lunch

Location: In the office

Monthly Bills

Rent: 1st of the month

Phone: 15th of the month

Credit card: 20th of the month

Location: _____

Location: _____

Location: _____

Location: _____

Weekly Warrior

Young adults can have several schedules to balance, and it's easy to get overwhelmed or miss something important if you are not organized. Creating lists is an easy way to prioritize your tasks and get it done! Using this chart, write down your main goals or tasks that you would like to tackle this week. This can include home tasks like organizing a room, work tasks like preparing for a presentation, or social tasks like planning an event. You can even try color-coding the types of events to help you prioritize even more. Then break down what items need to be accomplished each day. Feel the joy as you cross finished items off your list.

Weekly To-Dos

✓ _____

✓ _____

✓ _____

✓ _____

✓ _____

✓ _____

✓ _____

➡️

Monday

Tuesday

Wednesday

Thursday

Friday

Saturday/Sunday

Looking Ahead... Next Week To-Dos

_____ _____ _____

How Long Will It Take?

Being able to estimate time is a helpful skill that allows you to better balance the demands of your work and personal life. Use this activity to increase your awareness of time and to gain a better understanding of how long various tasks take to complete. Over the next week, estimate how long you think each of the following activities will take you. Then use a stopwatch or timer to record how long the activity actually takes. Review your findings with your clinician.

Task	Estimated Time to Complete	Actual Time to Complete
Traveling to work, school, or an appointment		
Running an errand (e.g., dry cleaning, mailing a package)		
Checking the weather forecast for the upcoming week		
Making a meal		
Completing a household task (e.g., cleaning, organizing)		
Add your own:		
Add your own:		
Add your own:		

On Time

Being on time to scheduled events can help you feel prepared, and it shows other people that you value their time as well. However, being able to manage time requires an understanding of how long a task will take from start to finish. Use this tool to help you estimate how long different activities will take. Identify what event you need to attend, how long you think it will take to get there, how long you anticipate the event will last, and any unexpected barriers that may affect your estimate.

For example, let's say you plan to meet a friend at the local coffee shop at 10 a.m. It takes 10 minutes to walk there, but you occasionally run into other acquaintances when you walk through the neighborhood. In this case, it's best to leave a few minutes early to give yourself a buffer in case you run into a friendly neighbor and have a brief chat.

What event do you need to go to?	What time should you arrive there?
How long will it take to get there?	How long do you think the event will last?
Are there any barriers that may make it take longer?	
Based on your answers, what time should you leave for this event?	

What event do you need to go to?	What time should you arrive there?
How long will it take to get there?	How long do you think the event will last?
Are there any barriers that may make it take longer?	
Based on your answers, what time should you leave for this event?	

Chunk It

Large projects or tasks can be overwhelming and leave you frozen, not knowing where or how to start. Chunking is a simple strategy to help alleviate the stress of large assignments. By breaking down large tasks into smaller, more manageable components, the assignment becomes less overwhelming. Think of a large project or task that you need to complete at home, school, or work. Let's chunk it to help you get it done!

Project or task:

Due date:

Time remaining:

Materials needed:

Chunk 1:

Deadline:

Chunk 2:

Deadline:

Chunk 3:

Deadline:

Chunk 4:

Deadline:

Schedule a Test Drive

There are many ways to keep track of your schedule, so it's important to find the right tool for you. In this activity, explore different methods you have used to manage your schedule in the past and any new methods you'd like to try going forward. Then take an intentional test drive by trying out a few methods to find out what works best for you.

Part 1: Explore Different Methods

Methods	Have Tried Before	Would Like to Try
Phone calendar		
Phone alarms		
Email calendar		
Daily planner		
Other:		
Other:		
Other:		

Part 2: Schedule a Test Drive

Select three different methods and give each one a week-long test drive. At the end of the week, reflect on your choice. Was this method easy to use? What did you like about it? Did you encounter any problems? At the end of your trial period, select your preferred method.

Week 1 choice: _____

Reflection: _____

_____

Week 2 choice: _____

Reflection: _____

_____

Week 3 choice: _____

Reflection: _____

_____

Preferred method: _____

Mindful Workspace

Whether you work from home, at an office, or at a desk at school, having a mindful, organized workspace can help you stay focused. Use this checklist to set up a workspace environment that provides you with a sense of structure and calm.

Mindful Workplace Checklist

Designate Your Space

- Find a designated office or school space

- Find a designated work-from-home space

Organize Your Space

- Find the materials you need (e.g., pens, paper, laptop, etc.)

- Make an organized space for the materials you need (e.g., drawer, utensil container, file folder)

Energize Your Space

- Find ways to create calming light (e.g., natural light or lamps instead of overhead lights)

- Introduce natural elements (e.g., a real or artificial plant)

Reduce Distractions

- Place distracting items, like your phone or tablet, away in a nearby area

- Consider the location of the room, including the visibility of doors and windows

Personalize Your Space

- Add a favorite picture, inspirational quote, or sign

- Add a few favorite items (just be careful not to clutter your space!)

A Place for Everything

Imagine you are running late, rushing to get out the door, and now you can't find your keys, wallet, or cell phone. What you are looking for might be nearby—maybe just in an unusual place—but either way, it can be very stressful. To help you avoid this situation, you can designate a space where you store all the essential items you need in your day. For example, maybe you place a small bowl by the entryway to keep your wallet. Or perhaps you install a hook by the front door to hang your keys. Whenever you leave or come home, make sure you place these items in that specified area so they are always accessible.

Use this worksheet to create a list of the essential items you need to keep track of each day, and designate a place to store them as part of your daily routine. First, identify what items you need to keep track of each day.

_____

_____

_____

Next, brainstorm different areas where can you store each of these items so you don't misplace them.

Home	Work/School	Other

A Place for Everything Practice

Now that you have identified your essential items and designated a place to store them, it is time to practice your routine. Practice makes perfect. For the next week, check yourself at the end of the day, and record whether or not you were successful in using your designated areas.

	I Was Able to Find My Essential Items	I Used My Designated Areas for My Items	Notes
Day 1			
Day 2			
Day 3			
Day 4			
Day 5			
Day 6			
Day 7			

At the end of the week, think about these questions:

Were your designated spaces helpful? If not, what changes can you make? _____

_____

Are there other items you need to add to your list? _____

_____

Autism Spectrum Disorder

Young adults with autism spectrum disorder have a range of strengths, as well as areas for growth, across social, communication, and behavioral domains. As these individuals strive for independence, it is key for them to learn ways to effectively advocate for themselves and interact with others.

The initial activities in this chapter provide a variety of strategies to highlight clients' unique strengths and to help them gain a greater understanding of how they perceive information from their environment. In addition, relationship coaching activities are included to strengthen clients' social confidence and to increase their ability to connect with others in adulthood. Resiliency activities bring greater awareness to expected and unexpected behaviors that clients may encounter across different settings. Finally, the mindful adaptation section includes activities that enhance clients' ability to adapt to change and learn ways to manage stress when life throws a curveball.

Cover Letter

Social scripts are helpful strategies that can help you become more confident with sharing information about yourself and communicating with others. Use this template to create your own cover letter, tailoring these statements as you see fit or adding some of your own. When you're done, this cover letter can serve as a visual reminder of information you can share with others to help increase connection and understanding.

Hello, my name is _____.

It's nice to meet you. I would like to share a little bit about myself.

My top three strengths are _____

_____.

I am really interested in _____.

And I would like to learn more about _____.

I think a bit differently than others at times, so please be patient.

When learning new skills or routines, I learn best by _____

_____.

I prefer to communicate by _____

_____.

At times, it is difficult for me to _____

_____.

To handle worry or stress, I like to _____

_____.

I look forward to (e.g., being a part of, working with, or learning more about) _____

_____.

Thank you for listening!

Thriving Thinker

As you transition into different stages of life, you will experience challenges, but you'll also have an opportunity to share your many talents with others. Use this tool to gain an awareness of your talents and to better understand what elements in your environment can help you thrive. Brainstorm your ideal ways of working and interacting with others, as well as real-life examples showing how you thrive. This will help you advocate for your needs as you adjust to new experiences as an adult.

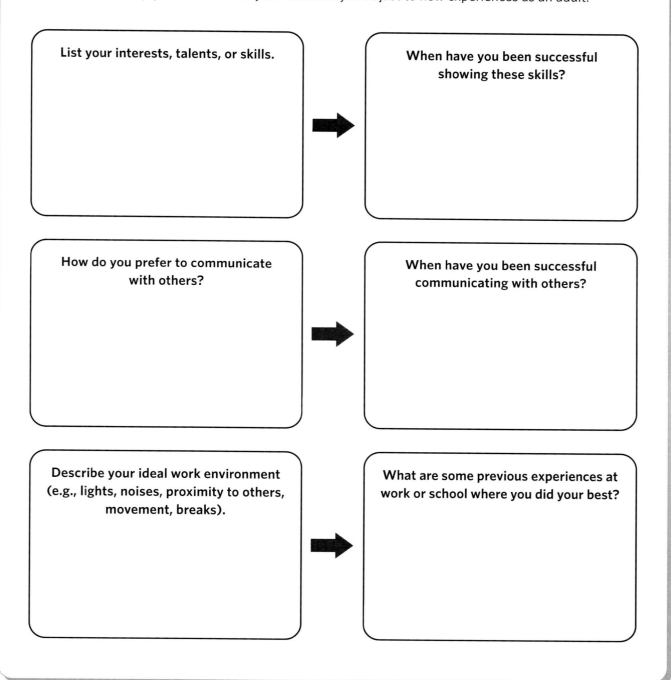

List your interests, talents, or skills.

When have you been successful showing these skills?

How do you prefer to communicate with others?

When have you been successful communicating with others?

Describe your ideal work environment (e.g., lights, noises, proximity to others, movement, breaks).

What are some previous experiences at work or school where you did your best?

Thriving Thinker:
Needs and Reminders

As an adult, you must learn to adapt to different settings at school, at work, and in your personal life. There will be times when you need to ask for accommodations to help you succeed (e.g., asking for clear expectations or extended timelines), as well as times when you will need to adjust to the setting even when it might be uncomfortable (e.g., sharing your ideas with a group, listening to others' ideas, trying something new).

How do you adjust to different settings in a way that allows you to thrive? With the help of your clinician, explore what accommodations can help you thrive and what reminders can help you be flexible when adapting to different settings.

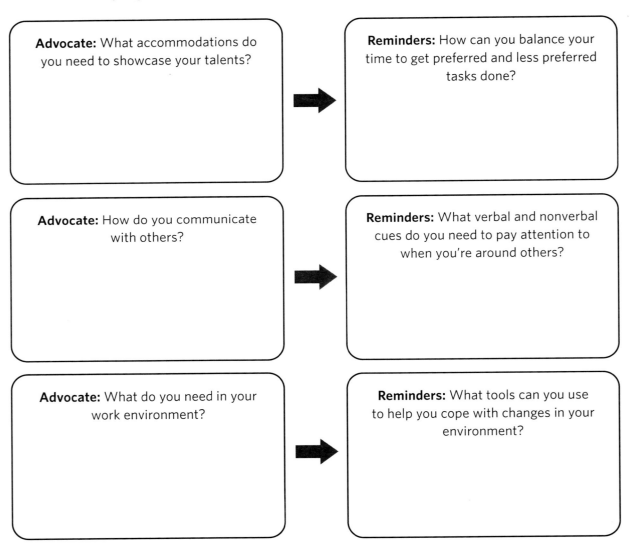

Advocate: What accommodations do you need to showcase your talents?

Reminders: How can you balance your time to get preferred and less preferred tasks done?

Advocate: How do you communicate with others?

Reminders: What verbal and nonverbal cues do you need to pay attention to when you're around others?

Advocate: What do you need in your work environment?

Reminders: What tools can you use to help you cope with changes in your environment?

Sensory Profile

We use our senses to gather information about our world. Each of us has unique sensory preferences, meaning that we all tolerate or prefer different levels of touch, sight, taste, sound, and smell. Use this chart to list your preferences and to define your limits for each of the senses. This tool can help you communicate and advocate for what you need at work, at school, or in the community.

	Just Right	Too Much
Touch		
Sight		
Smell		
Taste		
Sound		

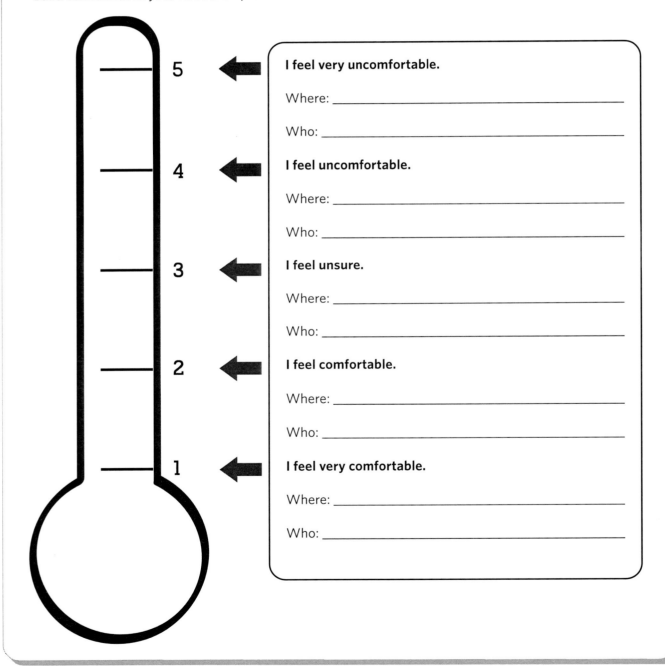

Social Comfort Scale

Healthy social relationships are an important part of adulthood, but it is normal to experience different comfort levels within varying social settings, depending on whether you're socializing with your friends, family, or colleagues. Starting at the bottom of this scale, identify social situations in which you are most comfortable and confident. Then continue moving up the scale to recognize other situations in which you are not as comfortable. Use on this tool often and adjust your ratings as you build confidence in your relationship skills.

5 ← **I feel very uncomfortable.**

Where: _____

Who: _____

4 ← **I feel uncomfortable.**

Where: _____

Who: _____

3 ← **I feel unsure.**

Where: _____

Who: _____

2 ← **I feel comfortable.**

Where: _____

Who: _____

1 ← **I feel very comfortable.**

Where: _____

Who: _____

Social Schedule

When you were a child, social activities—like playdates, sports teams, and birthday parties—were organized by the adults around you. But as you become older, there aren't always as many structured social routines or schedules, so it's possible to spend most of your time alone. Use this worksheet to brainstorm ways you can spend time with others who support you or who share similar interests. Here are a few simple ways to interact with others on a regular basis:

- Set a time each week to go for a walk with a friend.

- Sign up for a group class at the gym.

- Schedule a call or video conference with a family member.

- Join a social group to play a game or sport.

- Visit the local recreation center or library.

How can you build social time into your daily schedule? With your clinician, select a few social activities that fit your interests, and make it a point to integrate these into your schedule.

Social Activity	Who Will Be There?	How Often Will You Go?

Social Activity Log

As you move through the week, use this worksheet to log any social activities you engage in. Include a description of who was there and how comfortable you felt (with 1 being *very comfortable* and 5 being *very uncomfortable*). Then describe whether you think you would be interested in doing this activity again. At the end of the week, share this log with your clinician.

Activity	Who Was There?	Comfort Level (1–5)	Would You Do This Again? Why or Why Not?

Social Reminders

In-Session
Exercise

Think of social expectations or norms as those unwritten rules for interacting with others. These social expectations change to meet the needs of different settings. For instance, the way you interact with your friends is probably much more casual than the way you interact with your supervisor.

Can you recognize some of these unwritten rules for interacting across different settings? Some factors to consider are tone of voice, volume of voice, topics of conversation, and length of conversation—to name a few. To help you sort out these different social expectations, write down a few reminders in the chart provided. Notice which expectations overlap and which ones differ.

Friends and Family (Casual)

1. _____

2. _____

3. _____

Work or School (Professional)

1. _____

2. _____

3. _____

Community (Less Familiar)

1. _____

2. _____

3. _____

Confidence in Real Life

Confidence lies in our thoughts, feelings, and actions. As you face new adult hurdles in your personal and professional life, it is important to present yourself in a confident manner. Use this exercise to define what confidence means to you. Write down a current situation in which you showed confidence (or an upcoming situation where you want to be confident), and describe your confident thoughts, feelings, and actions.

Example:

Situation or event: Meeting a new boss or supervisor

Confident Thoughts	Confident Feelings	Confident Actions
I am a hard worker	Nervous but in control	Introduce myself with a clear voice and a firm handshake

Situation or event:

Confident Thoughts	Confident Feelings	Confident Actions

Situation or event:

Confident Thoughts	Confident Feelings	Confident Actions

Confident Communicator

In-Session
Exercise

Confident communicators present their body, voice, and ideas in a poised manner. They can share their ideas and personality while listening and respecting others' views. Although communication is a skill that can continue to grow with experience, there are many communication skills you already have. Review these key elements of effective communication. Then identify areas in which you already excel and areas where you can grow. When have you been a confident communicator?

Key elements of effective communication:

- Open-mindedness
- Respect
- Active listening
- Summary statements
- Asking others questions

- Empathy
- Clear and concise language
- Confidence
- Nonverbal skills
- Speaking at a conversational rate

- Approachableness
- Accepting feedback
- Tone of voice
- Asking questions
- Adjusting proximity to others

I am great at:

I am good at:

I am working on:

In-Session
Exercise

Communication Limits

What constitutes an appropriate topic of conversation changes as a function of the environment and social group around you. There are several factors to consider when thinking about topics of conversation, like who your audience is, their level of comfort, and the appropriateness of the topic given the situation. For instance, you can have more casual conversations with close friends and family, but you may need to be more guarded when talking with others you don't know as well, like colleagues or your supervisor at work. Create a list of conversation topics or information that would be acceptable to share with each group, as well as those that you may want to avoid.

Audience	Topics/Information to Share	Topics/Information to Avoid
Close family members		
Close friends		
Acquaintances (e.g., friends you do not know as well)		
Colleagues at work or school		
Supervisors, bosses, school faculty		
Clinical providers, case manager, medical staff, therapists, etc.		
Other:		
Other:		

I Noticed...

Facial expressions and body language are helpful nonverbal cues that can convey a range of feelings. Take notice of your own nonverbal cues and explore what you notice about other people's cues. Look in the mirror, watch your favorite show, and ask a trusted person to join in this activity with you. Then, using the chart, write down different nonverbal cues you notice in each category. What changes in nonverbals do you notice across these various emotional states?

I Noticed...	Sad	Calm or Happy	Stressed	Angry
Facial expressions				
Tone of voice				
Eye gaze				
Body language (e.g., hands, posture, legs, feet)				
Personal space (e.g., proximity to others)				

Choices

When big feelings emerge, there are many ways to handle them. Knowing that you have choices in these situations can make your feelings more manageable and help you feel empowered. Write down three strategies that can help you cope with each feeling listed here. Some strategies may work for several feelings, while others may not be as helpful. If you get stuck, ask a trusted friend, family member, or clinician to help you generate new ideas.

When I feel **confused**, I can:

Plan A: _____

Plan B: _____

Plan C: _____

When I feel **overly excited**, I can:

Plan A: _____

Plan B: _____

Plan C: _____

When I feel **upset**, I can:

Plan A: _____

Plan B: _____

Plan C: _____

When I feel **frantic**, I can:

Plan A: _____

Plan B: _____

Plan C: _____

When I feel **overwhelmed**, I can:

Plan A: _____

Plan B: _____

Plan C: _____

When I feel **angry**, I can:

Plan A: _____

Plan B: _____

Plan C: _____

My Go-To

Familiar people in our lives, like our family or friends, can help us when we need support. Who are the important people in your life? It is important to know whom you can reach out to (and how to do so) when you need support the most. List some of your trusted relationships here. Do you go to the same person or different people depending on the situation? List as many names as you would like. Do not stress if you cannot answer a question. Simply think of someone you might like to connect with in that way.

First, list all your trusted relationships (e.g., family, friends, partners, clinical supports, community supports): _____

_____

_____

_____

_____

_____

Whom are you comfortable talking to when you are lonely? _____

_____

Who makes you laugh? _____

_____

Who is a good listener? _____

_____

Whom can you trust with personal information or concerns? _____

_____

Who can help you problem solve? _____

_____

Who can cheer you up when you're feeling sad? _____

_____

My Responsibility Reminder

In-Session
Exercise

Life is full of stressful moments. Knowing what you can control in a situation—and what you have limited to no control over—can help you stay grounded. Use this activity as a helpful reminder of what you are responsible for and what you need to let go. Think of a stressful situation you are going through or have experienced in the past. What can you control? What do you need to let go of?

Can Control	Let Go
• My thoughts, words, and actions	• Others' thoughts, words, and actions
• My choices and mistakes	• Others' choices and mistakes
• My beliefs and values	• Others' beliefs
• How I treat myself	• Events and environment around me (e.g., weather, traffic)
• How I treat others	
• My effort	
• My attitude toward work, school, etc.	

Stressful situation:

Can Control	Let Go

Adjusting to Expectations

Part of being a successful adult is learning to adjust your actions to meet the expectations of the setting. For instance, at home or with friends, you can be casual in terms of how you act, dress, and speak. But at work or school, you need to present yourself in a professional manner, taking note of how you interact with others, what you talk about, and how you dress.

Use this worksheet to identify specific actions that are expected of you based on the setting (e.g., getting to work on time, raising your hand to speak in class) and those that would be less acceptable or unexpected (e.g., wearing pajamas to work, talking loudly about personal issues with colleagues).

At Home	
Expected	**Unexpected**

In Casual Settings with Friends	
Expected	**Unexpected**

At Work or School	
Expected	**Unexpected**

Sticky Situations

Whom do you ask for help when you feel stuck? When you were younger, you probably reached out to family, friends, and school staff when you had a problem. But as you grow older, you may turn to different people for help, and you will be expected to do more problem solving on your own. Some problems require the assistance of others, and some do not.

The next time you are in a sticky situation, first take a deep breath and assess the size of the problem. Then ask yourself if this has happened before and if it's something you can handle. If the problem seems out of reach, where can you find help? For example, if your bike tire popped, you could search the internet to learn how to change a bike tire, call a family member for their advice, or seek out a specialist at a bike repair shop. Read through the sample problems here and identify how to seek help for each.

Problem	Size of the Problem (Small, Medium, Major)	Who Can Help?	How Can You Ask for Help?
You accidentally delete an email with important due dates from your professor or supervisor.			
You get lost on a walk around your new neighborhood.			
You are really upset about feedback you received on a project.			
You accidentally hit a car in the parking lot.			
You lose your ID (e.g., driver's license, school or work badge).			
Other:			

Pocket of Sunshine

Everyone can use a little reminder of how wonderful they are. Take a minute to fill this card with words or phrases that describe all your strengths and positive attributes. Place this card in a location where you will see it often. In fact, make a few copies to place around your home, in your car, or at work—wherever it may brighten your day.

You are amazing!

Next Steps

There are a number of major milestones when it comes to achieving independence as an adult, like starting a new job, moving into your own place, or going to college. However, these accomplishments sometimes come with worries that overshadow the excitement you feel. The key is to balance your hesitation with your eager anticipation for the adventures ahead. Use this activity to help you express your worries while also recognizing all you have accomplished (or are excited to accomplish) in achieving this next step. Then identify ways you can prepare for any potential problems. An example is provided for you first.

Event: Starting a new job

Potential Problems

I need to find out how to get to work.

I must wake up at a different time.

I won't know anyone at my new job.

Your Accomplishments/ What You Are Excited For

I interviewed and got the job!

I communicated my talents in a professional way.

I will learn new skills.

I will meet others with similar interests.

How might you solve these potential problems? I can locate the right bus route and practice once before I start. I will set my alarm a day early to see what it's like to wake up at a different time. I can introduce myself when I get to work.

Event: _____

Potential Problems

Your Accomplishments/ What You Are Excited For

How might you solve these potential problems? _____

_____

_____

Settings and Strategies

Isn't it frustrating when wireless devices like your headphones disconnect when you're in a meeting or listening to music? In these situations, a typical, expected response would be to take a deep breath and resync your device. A less typical, unexpected response might be to throw your headphones, yell, or put your head down. There are times in real life when routines change. When these unexpected changes occur, it is helpful to reset with the use of coping tools. Remember: You may have more freedom to reboot in your home than you do at work or in the community. In this activity, work with your clinician to brainstorm some helpful coping tools you can use to match the setting. Circle any coping skills you can use across multiple settings, and underline any that are specific to just one setting. Add to your lists as you uncover strategies that work for you.

Home

School/Work

Community

Add Your Own

Change of Plans!

Routines provide structure and predictability to daily life. They provide comfort because you know what to expect. What happens when those plans change without notice and you need problem-solving skills to navigate challenges on the fly? Although it's easy to panic, that won't solve the problem. Think about each of the scenarios provided here, and brainstorm ways to solve the problem, either by adapting or by asking for help.

1. Imagine you take the bus to work every day, but today it doesn't show up. What do you do?

   _____

   _____

2. Imagine you head to the cafeteria after class to purchase your favorite cheeseburger. It's so good you eat it every day. Today the menu changed, and your burger is not available. What do you do?

   _____

   _____

3. Imagine you schedule an appointment with your dentist, but when you arrive, there is someone new filling in for the day. What do you do?

   _____

   _____

4. Imagine you have waited all week to meet a friend for dinner, but your plans change at the last minute due to bad weather. What do you do?

   _____

   _____

5. Imagine you show up at your local gym to use the treadmill. You arrive at the same time every day and use the same machine. Today someone else is using that machine. What do you do?

   _____

   _____

Anger and Related Behavior Disorders

It is natural to experience anger or irritability in response to situations where we perceive that fairness or justice has been compromised. However, intense and prolonged anger can lead people to engage in destructive actions toward themselves and others. It can also result in serious consequences when it comes to forming and maintaining relationships, as well as succeeding at work or school.

Therefore, the activities in this section provide clients with several opportunities to learn more about their experience of anger and gain greater awareness of their anger triggers. In addition, relationship coaching activities provide clients with tools to increase empathy and improve their ability to take the perspective of others. Resiliency building activities are also included to support the growth of critical skills like taking responsibility, apologizing, and staying in control. Finally, this chapter concludes with mindfulness tools that clients can use to redirect their anger into positive outlets and stay focused on what is important.

Getting Acquainted:
In Control vs. Out of Control

Working with your clinician, answer these questions to develop a personal understanding of what it feels like to be in control versus out of control.

1. Write down three words that describe being *in control* to you.

   _____   _____   _____

2. Describe a recent situation where you were confident and in control.

   • Where did it take place? _____

   • What happened? _____

   • Who was there? _____

   • How did this make you feel? _____

   • How did your body feel? _____

   • What helped you be successful in this situation? _____

     _____

3. Write down three words that describe feeling *out of control* to you.

   _____   _____   _____

4. Describe a recent situation where you felt angry and out of control.

   • Where did it take place? _____

   • What happened? _____

   • Who was there? _____

   • How did this make you feel? _____

   • How did your body feel? _____

   • What triggered you to react with anger in this situation? _____

     _____

5. How often do you feel in control during the week?

   Not at all   *Sometimes*   *Often*   *Most of the time*   *All the time*

6. How often do you feel out of control or angry during the week?

   Not at all   *Sometimes*   *Often*   *Most of the time*   *All the time*

7. List three strategies that help you stay in control during upsetting situations.

   - _____

   - _____

   - _____

Detecting Differences

There are over 3,000 words in our vocabulary that can be used to describe emotions. How many emotion words can you come up with? Try this two-part activity to gauge your ability to identify and describe different emotions. Work independently or with a partner to complete this activity.

Part 1: Emotion Minute

How many emotions can you list in one minute? Write them here.

Part 2: Defining Differences

What is the difference between these emotions? Work with a partner, use a dictionary, or search the internet for examples and definitions.

Example: Angry vs. disappointed: We feel angry when we believe an injustice has occurred, whereas we feel disappointed when someone does not live up to our expectations.

1. Excited vs. elated: _____

   _____

   _____

   _____

2. Angry vs. frustrated: _____

   _____

   _____

   _____

3. Sad vs. melancholy: _____

   _____

   _____

   _____

4. Annoyed vs. agitated: _____

   _____

   _____

   _____

5. Upset vs. uncertain: _____

   _____

   _____

   _____

Frustrated Feelings and Responses

Angry feelings, like frustration, come in a range of sizes and experiences that are unique to each of us. In this activity, describe different situations that cause you to feel varying levels of frustration, and notice how your body responds as a result (e.g., changes in breathing, sweating, movement, eating, sleeping, or concentration). Then create a short list of coping strategies that you can use depending on the level of frustration you are feeling. Remember, there are no right or wrong answers because this is based on your personal experience.

Level of Frustration	Example Situation	Body Reactions	Coping Tools I Can Use When I Feel This Way
Extreme frustration			
A lot of frustration			
Some frustration			
A little frustration			
Very little frustration			

Anger and Frustration Log

Homework Assignment

Over the next week, use this log to keep track of events that cause you stress, frustration, or even anger. Describe the event, and rate your level of frustration (1 = *very little frustration*, 5 = *extreme frustration*). List any thoughts that contributed to these emotions, and describe how your body responded (e.g., tight muscles, headache, sweating, changes in breathing). Finally, list any coping tools that you used. Remember that each experience is different. Share this information with your clinician to discuss your experience.

Event	Level of Frustration (1-5)	Angry or Frustrating Thoughts	Body Response	Coping Tools Used

■ 177

Power of Empathy

Empathy is the power to understand and share in someone else's experience. It is an important skill for building relationships with others in your personal life and work life. Use this tool to describe what empathy means to you. Then provide examples of how your actions, words, and thoughts can demonstrate empathy toward others.

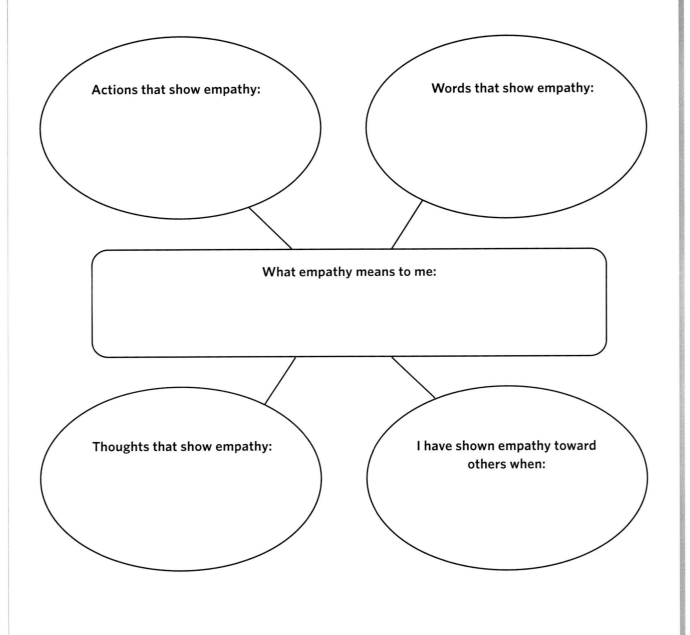

Family, Friends, and Colleagues

Take a minute to think about the relationships in your life, including family members, friends, and colleagues who are important to you. In the circles, list those important individuals with whom you have a trusted relationship and with whom you feel most comfortable. In the overlapping areas, list the common traits that these individuals share. Common traits might include compassionate, good listener, dependable, or kind.

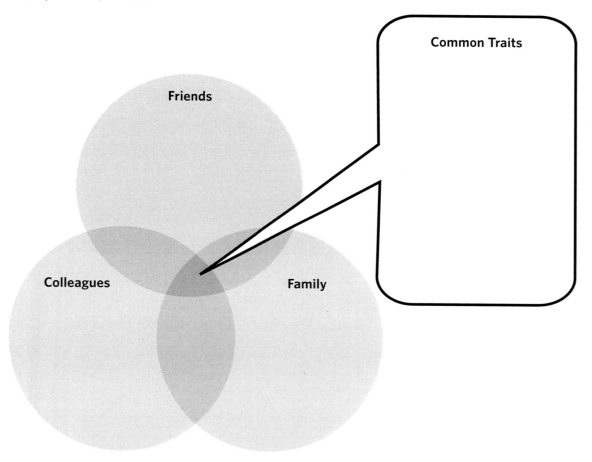

What traits do you have in common with others you trust? _____

_____

Select a trait that you share. Describe how you can show this trait in your actions with others.

_____

Admit and Act

Words and actions can have consequences that require you to take responsibility. In these moments, you need to acknowledge your role in the situation (*admit*) and own up to your mistake (*act*) by offering an apology and modifying your actions in the future. Taking responsibility can be difficult, but it is an important step for success in adulthood. Use this activity to consider some different situations in which you may need to admit wrongdoing and take responsibility.

Example

Situation: You show up late to a meeting because you overslept.

Say: "I'm sorry for being late. Your time is also valuable."

Make a change: Set an additional alarm or have a friend call you in the morning as a reminder.

Situation: After an argument with a friend, you recap the situation on social media and blame your friend.

Say: _____

Make a change: _____

Situation: You receive negative feedback on a project. You become defensive and make excuses for your performance.

Say: _____

Make a change: _____

Situation: _____

Say: _____

Make a change: _____

Situation: _____

Say: _____

Make a change: _____

My People

Who are your trusted people? These are people with whom you can share personal experiences, feel safe around, and be your authentic self. You may have one person or a few. Consider family, friends, mentors, or other important connections in your life. There are no right or wrong answers to these questions.

Whom can you have serious discussions with?	**Whom can you share fun times with?**	**Whom can you be vulnerable with?**

Who holds you accountable?	**Who practices self-care with you (e.g., walking or yoga partner)?**	**Who is always there for you in hard times?**

Who accepts you for who you are?	**Whom can you reach out to for advice?**	**Whom can you celebrate good news with?**

My Apologies

Making mistakes is part of the journey to adulthood. When mistakes occur, it is important to apologize and accept responsibility. Part of apologizing or admitting fault is taking into consideration your audience. If the issue is small, apologies can be informal as long as they are sincere—for example, through a quick conversation or even a text (though that's not the most personable choice). But if the issue is more serious or involves a more formal audience, like your colleagues or supervisors, your actions should match the setting to show your sincerity regarding the issue.

How many different ways can you say that you are sorry?

Words	Actions

How might an apology look with different groups of people? Notice similarities and differences in your words and actions in each situation.

Friends	Family	Colleagues	Supervisors, Bosses, Teachers, etc.

Check Engine

Just like a car has warning signals when the engine is overheating or the gas is low, our bodies give us signs when anger is on the rise. These signs may involve a change in *physical symptoms* (e.g., increased heart rate, rapid breathing, muscle tension, perspiration), a change in *feelings* (e.g., feeling irritable, vulnerable, or short-tempered), a change in *thoughts* (e.g., the belief that you are being treated unfairly or being threatened, or all-or-nothing thinking, like "This always happens to me"), or a change in *behaviors* (e.g., avoiding or withdrawing from others). Use this activity to gain awareness of your anger warning signs.

My Anger Warning Signs			
Physical Symptoms	**Feelings**	**Thoughts**	**Behaviors**

Warning Signs and Responses

When the gas light comes on in your car, you should take that as a hint to adjust your schedule and head to the gas station. You can only run on fumes for so long. The same applies to your warning signs for anger. By recognizing your warning signs, you can prepare coping strategies to help you manage your feelings more confidently and stay in control. Use this exercise to brainstorm tools you can use when your warning signs emerge.

Warning Signs		
Physical	• Tight muscles • Breathing faster • Getting red in the face • Feeling hot	• Talking faster • Talking louder • Pacing • Feeling restless
Mental	• Difficulty focusing • Feeling on edge • Ruminating on the situation • Predicting the worst	• Feeling like you have a "short fuse" with others • Feeling impatient • Making assumptions

What strategies work best to help make anger more manageable? Shade in those that apply or add your own.

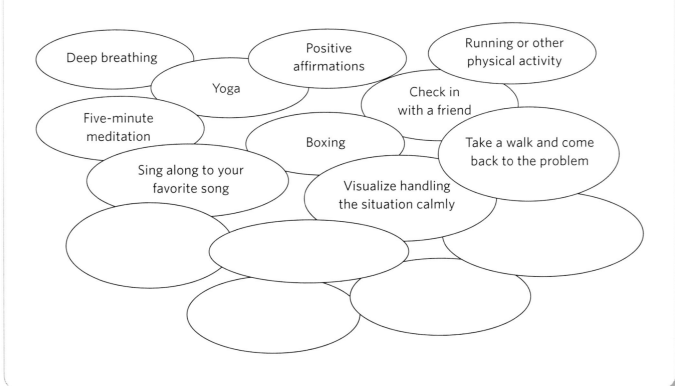

Before It's Too Late

When left unchecked, stress, irritation, and anger can build up in your body. It's important to know when you need to release these emotions so you don't hit your breaking point and act in a way that you later regret. Use this activity to learn how to notice when your anger is building and to identify tools that will help you keep your cool before it's too late.

TOO LATE!
Driving too fast after arguing with a friend

TOO LATE!
After a frustrating call, slamming your phone down and cracking the screen

TOO LATE!
Yelling at a coworker when they accidentally bump into you

Body signals to look for:

Thoughts and feelings to look for:

Actions you can take before it's too late:

Success Planning

Anger is a normal reaction to situations in which you feel wronged, misunderstood, or disrespected. However, when anger becomes too intense, it can lead to verbal or physical outbursts that take away from your productivity. Acknowledging different situations that may trigger your anger is an important step in making it more manageable.

Create a plan to help make anger more manageable in your personal life, your work or school life, and your community. First think about triggers or problems you may encounter in each setting and write them in the circles.

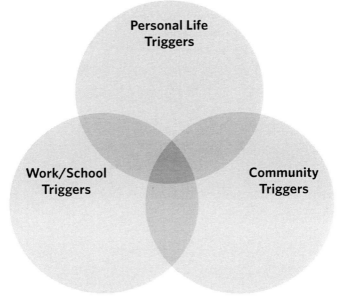

Then list strategies that can help you stay in control in each of these settings. Highlight or circle strategies that can be helpful across settings.

Personal Life	Work/School Life	Community Life

Beneficial Behaviors

Beneficial behaviors are prosocial actions that can help you build relationships with others, work cooperatively, and handle tough situations with success. Look at the situations here, and brainstorm helpful actions you could engage in to build a relationship with that person. How can you transfer these experiences to upcoming challenges you may encounter at home, at work or school, or in the community?

Situation	Helpful Actions	Possible Outcomes
A new employee starts work today, and their desk is next to yours.	Introduce yourself Offer to eat lunch together	Make the new employee feel comfortable Make a new connection at work
It is raining outside, and your elderly neighbor is trying to get their groceries to their apartment.		
You notice that a colleague is wearing a baseball hat of your favorite sports team.		
Add your own:		
Add your own:		
Add your own:		

Defusing Angry Energy

Anger is a normal feeling, but how we respond to and handle that feeling is important. The key to managing anger is to find helpful coping strategies that make you less physically and emotionally reactive to the situation. Here are a few ideas:

- Focus on what you can control. Ask yourself, "Can I change the situation? Can I leave the situation? Can I see the situation from another viewpoint?"

- Try "I" statements rather than "you" statements: "I feel _____ when _____ because _____. What I need is _____."

- Give yourself time to problem solve so you are reacting with reason rather than emotion.

- Remove yourself from the situation.

- Reflect on the situation later. Ask the other person, "Can we talk about this tomorrow?"

- Let thoughts come and go with brief breathing or meditation exercises.

- Take notice of your anger triggers. Ask yourself, "What is it about this situation that is making me so angry?"

Let's practice! Imagine these scenarios made you feel angry. What could you do to defuse your anger in each situation?

1. You confide in a friend about a personal matter, but you find out that they broke your trust and told others.

   _____

   _____

2. You get cut off in traffic by someone who didn't use their turn signal, and you have to hit your brakes.

   _____

   _____

3. A family member tries to tell you how to run your life.

   _____

   _____

4. You feel you are pushed aside when asking for help at work.

_____

_____

5. You pull your car over to fix a flat tire, and a passing car speeds through a puddle, splashing you. You are late for work and completely soaked.

_____

_____

6. In front of others, you are told that you did something wrong.

_____

_____

Patient Response

Difficult or challenging situations in life can create intense feelings. You may want to react right away to get out your frustration, but that's not always the best solution. Practice patience by comparing a quick response to a patient response. For each of the scenarios provided, think about how you might respond immediately compared to how you might respond if you took a minute to pause first. How might you communicate your feelings in a different way?

1. **Situation:** Your friend shows up 45 minutes late to your lunch outing.

   Answer now: _____

   _____

   Wait a minute: _____

   _____

2. **Situation:** Your supervisor gives you feedback on a project that you disagree with.

   Answer now: _____

   _____

   Wait a minute: _____

   _____

3. **Situation:** Your ex posts a picture of their new partner on social media.

   Answer now: _____

   _____

   Wait a minute: _____

   _____

4. **Situation:** Your neighbor leaves a note at your door to complain that your pet is barking or your music is playing too loudly.

   Answer now: _____

   _____

   Wait a minute: _____

   _____

Anger Outlets

Anger is an intense emotion that can create equally intense physical energy. What do you do with your angry energy? A helpful way to handle angry energy is to find activities to help relieve this energy. In this activity, think of ways to move your energy into different outlets or activities that are physical, creative, problem-solving, and mindful. Review the suggestions and add your own ideas. And remember, it is most helpful to brainstorm ideas when you are feeling calm.

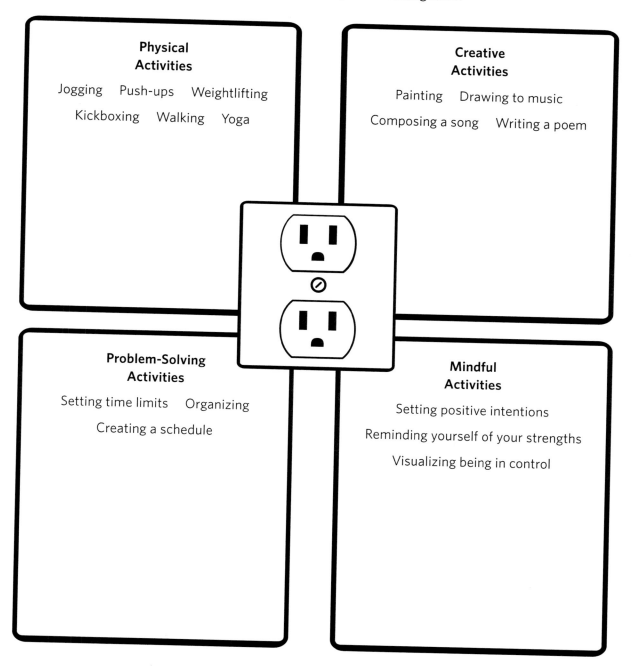

Physical Activities

Jogging   Push-ups   Weightlifting

Kickboxing   Walking   Yoga

Creative Activities

Painting   Drawing to music

Composing a song   Writing a poem

Problem-Solving Activities

Setting time limits   Organizing

Creating a schedule

Mindful Activities

Setting positive intentions

Reminding yourself of your strengths

Visualizing being in control

Get Grounded

When you're faced with an anger-provoking situation, it can be difficult to keep your cool. Grounding is a helpful technique to connect with your body and let go for a moment. It helps calm the body and allow you to move forward. Try this grounding activity the next time you feel anger emerging. Identify what is bothering you, then use your senses to ground yourself in the present moment. When you are done, reset and focus on how you can tackle what is bother you in a helpful way.

What is bothering you?

_____

_____

Take a deep breath in, exhale, and get grounded:

What are FIVE sounds you hear?

What are FOUR things you see?

What are THREE things you smell?

What are TWO things you feel?

Take ONE deep breath in and then exhale.

Now what can you do about what is bothering you?

_____

_____

_____

Follow Your Arrow

An arrow is a symbol that is used to provide directions on maps, on instruction sheets, on buildings—basically everywhere. Design your own arrows to guide you toward your goals. In each arrow, write down an inspirational saying from your favorite author, songwriter, or other famous person. Place these arrows in a high-traffic area—like your room, your daily planner, or your car—to remind you of your intentions and purpose.

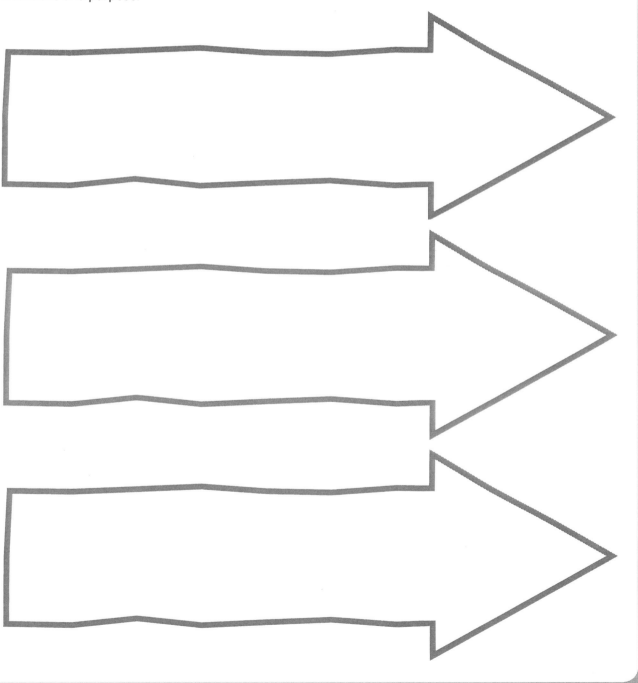

Kudos!

Give yourself credit for the efforts you make each day. Some days you will do big, amazing things like solving a problem at work or finishing a home improvement project. Other days you will accomplish small yet meaningful tasks, like eating healthy, doing a favor for a friend, or arriving to work on time. What did you do today that deserves a compliment? Whatever it is, pat yourself on the back. Adulting is not easy, but small efforts can help you be successful.

Monday	Tuesday	Wednesday

Thursday		Friday

Saturday	Sunday

About the Author

Lisa Weed Phifer, DEd, NCSP, is a trauma-informed social-emotional learning (SEL) specialist and nationally certified school psychologist, holding additional certifications in cognitive behavioral therapy (CBT), autism, and youth mental health. Phifer's work integrates CBT and core social-emotional competencies into practical, child-focused activities. She has an extensive list of publications and has presented across the U.S. and internationally to educators, clinicians, and parents. Her most rewarding role is at home with her husband, Jeffrey, daughter, Genevieve, and double doodles, Midas and Hobart.